Retu

Return to the Promised Land

THE STORY OF OUR SPIRITUAL RECOVERY

Grant R. Schnarr

CHRYSALIS BOOKS

Imprint of the Swedenborg Foundation

West Chester, Pennsylvania

Chrysalis Books is an imprint of the Swedenborg Foundation, Inc. For more information, contact:

Chrysalis Books
The Swedenborg Foundation
320 N. Church Street
West Chester, PA 19380

Library of Congress Cataloging-in-Publication Data

Schnarr, Grant R.
  Return to the promised land : the story of our spiritual recovery / by Grant R. Schnarr.
      p.   cm.
  Includes bibliographical references.
  ISBN 0-87785-179-4 (alk. paper)
    1. Spiritual life.   2. Jews—History—to 1200 B.C.   3. Bible. O.T.
  Exodus—Criticism, interpretation, etc.   I. Title.
BV4501.2.S2962   1997   96–46221
248.4—dc21   CIP

Cover illustration: *June Skies (A Perfect Day)* by Maxfield Parrish. Photo courtesy of the Archives of the American Illustrators Gallery, New York City. ©1996, by ASap of Holderness, NH, 032045, USA. Authorized by the Maxfield Parrish Family Trust.

Designed by Omega Clay
Edited by Mary Lou Bertucci
Typeset in Fournier by Braun-Brumfield, Inc.

For Mom and Dad

Contents

Introduction: *My Journey*

I have surely seen the oppression of my people who are in Egypt, and have heard their cry because of their taskmasters, for I know their sorrows. So I have come down to deliver them out of the hand of the Egyptians, and to bring them up from that land to a good and large land, to a land flowing with milk and honey.

EXODUS 3:7-8

I invite you to come with me on a journey. The path we will travel is not new. In many ways this is an ancient journey first taken thousands of years ago by a group of people seaching for a home. But every person—of whatever time, and background, and religious orientation—is called to this journey on a spiritual level. God, as we understand him, calls you and me out of the slavery of egotism and mistaken wants, out of addiction, in whatever form that may take, to freedom. I ask you to adventure with me, to leave the old ways behind, and to search for a new and promised way of life, what many call "the road to recovery" and what the Israelites called the "return to the promised land."

Before you agree to embark on this journey, you probably want to know more about me, about my experience in taking this kind of journey, and whether I can get you to where we want to go. That's why I want to share with you my credentials, my badges, and achievements. And then I want to tell you what is really important about myself.

About my accomplishments: When I was a young man I won two different medals for good citizenship and scholarship. I was president of the local boys' club and later president of my fraternity in high school. I was graduated from college with a bachelor of religion degree and went on to get a master's degree in theology, and was ordained as a minister in my church. I am a minister in a very reasonable Christian church called the New Church, which believes that God is love, that people should be free to pursue God as they choose, that there is good in every religion, and that spiritual growth is a process, not something that happens in an instant with some sort of confession of faith. I also founded a local church congregation for the young at heart in Chicago and am the director of evangelization for the worldwide General Church of the New Jerusalem.

Over the past twelve years I've learned a lot about spiritual growth and recovery. I've counseled many people who are dealing with various challenges in addiction, marital difficulties, dysfunctional sexual behavior, bereavement, and a variety of other human challenges. Having been the pastor of a small church, I have been with people through their life changes, their children's births, marriages, and their deaths; and I have both celebrated and cried with them.

I am also a published author, who took the twelve-step program of Alcoholics Anonymous and made it accessible to everyone for their spiritual growth. My first book is called *Unlocking Your Spiritual Potential: A Twelve-Step Approach.* Groups have used this book as a basis for their spiritual growth in gatherings throughout the United States, Canada, Australia, England, Korea, and South Africa. This list of accomplishments might give some readers a sense that I may have something useful to say about spiritual growth. But I'd like to tell you some other things about my life that may present a different picture.

When I was a child, I used to block the closet doors of my room to stop the monsters from coming out at night. Sometimes they would still come out from other places. I remember slamming the bedroom door to block out the shouting coming from the other room and collapsing into a corner confused and afraid of the world.

My younger sister and I would often grab a piece of bread from the kitchen, and mix up a quick concoction to go with it before slipping into our bedroom. We'd rub the white bread between our hands into tiny balls, like the bread from heaven in the Bible, and mix up a bowl of ketchup and vinegar, like the vinegar Jesus had to drink when he was crucified. We'd hide between the two twin beds and reenact Jesus' Last Supper. We would gently dip the bread into the bittersweet mixture and quietly repeat Jesus' words, "Lo, I am with you always, even unto the end of the world," as we raised the bread to our mouths and ate.

As alcoholics go, my father wasn't as destructive as many can be. But alcoholism certainly created some major problems for my family. I remember a lot of yelling, but I recall no physical violence or abuse. I just remember a lot of yelling. That makes sense. My last name, "Schnarr," is German. It means "disturber of the peace." So you know what kind of heredity exists in our family. We certainly wouldn't be accused of suppressing feelings. My father is now a recovering alcoholic going on his second decade of sobriety. My mother is a courageous and sweet woman who always cared for my four sisters and me, even in the bleakest of times. I am thankful for both of my parents. Today they are together in old age, working, growing, loving so many in so many ways. But they worked through a lot to get to where they are now. It wasn't always like that. Early on, despite their efforts to keep things together through the dysfunction the alcoholic years I remember in my childhood were often frightening and uncertain. As a child I really thought about God a lot, and talked to him often, and felt he was there for me more often than not, even when life seemed to get crazy, or even when I would run astray.

I started smoking cigarettes when I was nine years old and stealing booze when I was twelve. I became the leader of a large gang of suburban kids who would regularly burglarize homes for their stock of hard liquor. We'd drink on the local ballfield all night. Some kids got so sick that they fell unconscious and lost control of their bowels. We would ride it out with them until morning and carry them home. I remember carrying my best friend into the early light of sunrise telling him to hold on. Home was just over the hill into the light. No one ever died, but some came close. Not much sex took place in those early days, but some of us were sexually abused by an older teen who would occasionally show up to pick a boy of his choosing. It was twenty years later when I realized that he and another older boy had sexually abused me. I had talked my way out of what he wanted to do, but he still did enough to let me never forget those few moments of humiliation and pain. I still deal with the anger, and all that comes with it, from time to time.

I drank like an alcoholic, starting with my first drink as a child. I remember, at the age of thirteen, walking home from school at 4:00 P.M. in the afternoon, just finishing up a day of school, stomach twisted, heart fluttering, throat constricted, dying for a drink. I drank my way through high school and college and theological school, and somehow managed to "fool everyone," and even get above-average grades. During this time, I worked several summer jobs as a hard-hat worker, digging ditches in Raleigh, North Carolina, and running a backhoe and a tunnel-boring machine in Fairfax, Virginia. In whatever I did, I worked hard in the day and partied hard in the evening. I will spare you the rest of my war story with alcohol, but will tell you that I decided to get help many years later. Three months after being ordained as a minister, I woke up one morning and decided to quit. I didn't want alcohol to interfere with my efforts to be helpful to others. How could I guide people on a spiritual path if I wasn't on one myself? I got help through Alcoholics Anonymous and began my journey from the slavery of addiction.

I must confess that leaving the initial bondage was easy. I had seen enough plagues come into my life, into my relationship with my wife, children, friends, and also in my occupation, that leaving the addiction of alcohol behind was a relief and a spiritual experience in itself. But finding peace of mind in the wilderness was a difficult task. Peeling off layers of addictions, I found more potential addictions. Adult-child issues emerged, tendencies toward workaholism, love and relationship addiction, food addiction, and even being addicted to counseling followed. One by one these enemies presented themselves before me on my battlefield. Some came only in a show of force, retreating as quickly as they came. Other enemies attacked from behind, catching me by surprise. It took a lot of soul-searching and spiritual labor and combat to remove these barriers to having a happy, healthy life. But I did so. I learned much about God and spiritual growth at this time, not so much from the books, but from the struggle itself.

Through the search for wholeness and my own "promised land" I found him. God, as I understand him, lifted me up time and again, and protected me, fed me in my wilderness search, and brought me to spiritual recovery. I now enjoy this recovery one day at a time, and thank God for the help he gives me each day. Not only do I feel free, but I can see so clearly that I have learned from the pain and the struggle. I thank God for the new revelations he gives me each day about my life and for the continual reminders of his presence in the world around me. I thank him for the peace of mind I now often feel and for the deep delight and the pain of love. I am alive! Though I do not claim to know what tomorrow will bring, I know that just for today I will be happy. This present moment truly is eternity. I am in the perfect place at the perfect time, one day at a time.

So, I've been there. But why write a book? When I discovered the spiritual programs available to twelve-steppers and others dealing with spiritual challenges and addictions, I was amazed at how similar they were to what I had learned in my religion. My religion is based on the teachings of the eighteenth-century scientist and theologian Emanuel Swedenborg. He had always reported in his books that there were steps to spiritual growth and that people couldn't change on their own, but needed a higher power he called God. He taught in his books that people needed to examine themselves, or take what we call in AA "a moral inventory," to find out what they were like inside, and to pray to God to remove any character defects, one defect at a time. I was stunned to see the similarities.

Every time I opened my mouth in a meeting people would say, "Hey, where are you getting that information? That's amazing!" It was a little odd telling them it came from an eighteenth-century Swedish scientist, but that's where it came from. The ideas I learned from Swedenborg helped me to see why the spiritual-growth programs so many had adopted were so successful, and how to understand them and employ them more effectively.

The idea for this book came when I saw clearly that Swedenborg was getting these teachings from the Bible. This wasn't in any ordinary way. He claimed that the Bible had a deeper symbolic meaning that had to do with our own lives. As one literal story was told about the struggle of a nation, another story was being told about our own struggles. Swedenborg said, "The reason why the Word shines and is translucent . . . is because there is a spiritual and celestial meaning in every particular of the Word, and these meanings are in the light of heaven, so that through these meanings and by their light the Divine flows into . . . human beings" (*Doctrine of the Sacred Scripture* 58).[1] I was beginning to perceive this. In fact, as I studied Swedenborg and worked on my own spiritual life, I saw that the particular story of the Exodus was about me and everyone who is involved in recovery. I saw that the story of a people escaping the slavery of Egypt, wandering a wilderness in search of food and water, and eventually finding and conquering a land promised to them long ago was about the human struggle in general. I was on a journey, as we all are, to find wholeness and spirituality. I was searching for answers, being led and often fed by a divine force, and

---

1. Emanuel Swedenborg, *Doctrine of the Sacred Scripture*, in *Four Doctrines* (West Chester, PA: Swedenborg Foundation, 1997). As is standard in Swedenborg studies, the number following the title refers to a paragraph number, rather than to a page number, which is consistent in all editions.

I faced real enemies that needed to be conquered. I had to enter my own promised land of spiritual health and recovery. I realized that this applies to everyone who desires to begin a journey to leave behind his or her ego and addictions and find a new spirituality.

I started a series of talks on the subject for people at my church and then began to speak at larger gatherings of people coming together for mutual support for their spiritual growth. I talked about the slavery of Egypt as being an inner bondage that brings on its own plagues. I talked about the miracles the Israelites witnessed in the wilderness and how that related to the real miracles individuals witness as they wander their own paths of life. I spoke of the strategies the Israelites used to conquer the promised land and how, on a spiritual level, these strategies can be used by every person today to combat inner foes, such as fears, character defects, bad habits, and even dark evils in one's life. People would come to me and say, "I've heard the Bible before, but never like this. These stories are alive! You're pulling all kinds of truth right out of these stories!" I would always answer them by saying, "I'm not doing anything except showing what is already there. Swedenborg has found the key to understanding these stories, and the stories, when read as an allegory for spiritual growth, do their own teaching." Several people encouraged me time and again to write a book about these things. And so I did.

This particular book, *Return to the Promised Land,* is about the parable of the children of Israel's struggle to become a nation. By "parable," I mean a symbolic representation of our own human existence. This book does not merely offer a loose correlation between the history of a people and our own personal lives. It assigns each significant person, place, tree, rock, body of water, and stick in the hand a specific spiritual meaning that corresponds directly to our spiritual growth. Some of these meanings will be obvious and will make immediate sense. Others may surprise you at first, but you will soon see a pattern develop that brings home the point again and again: this story was written for you and me, for our spiritual development. It will soothe and encourage you to know that, even as God did not abandon his people so many thousands of years ago, he does not abandon his people today, but leads each one of us, if we will let him, to happiness and inner peace.

As your guide on this journey, I want you to know that I have taken and *am* taking this same journey daily. I firmly believe that you will learn a great deal about your personal spiritual journey from these descriptive biblical stories, from their deeper meaning brought to light by Emanuel Swedenborg, and from my own experience with pain, with life, and with growth. Preceding each chapter are biblical passages (all taken from the New King James Edition) that will be explicated, and I encourage you to delve into their symbolic meaning in your own life. Each chapter begins with a quotation from a work by Swedenborg, which was the starting point of my own interpretation; and ends with simple, practical exercises intended to help you put your newfound knowledge into immediate action. It is my hope that *Return to the Promised Land* will guide you from addiction to freedom, from spiritual hunger and thirst to being filled and never thirsting again, from the fury of inner spiritual warfare to lasting spiritual peace.

In my own journey through life and through the writing of this book, I've been helped by many people. I thank my wife Cathy for her support, in both her inspiration and her willingness to carry an extra load so that I could pursue this goal; also Laurie Volocyk and Gail Steiner for their work in keeping the ship sailing smoothly on the workfront; Elizabeth Schnarr and Rachel Fiske for their grammatical editing; and Ray Silverman and Erik Buss for their helpful editorial comments.

Most importantly, this book could not have been conceived or written without knowledge of the works of Emanuel Swedenborg (1688-1772). His books have unlocked the Bible for me and have allowed me to enter into it, on a genuine spiritual journey to find my Maker.

Return to the Promised Land

The Lord appeared to Abram and said to him, "I am the Almighty God; walk before me and be blameless. And I will make my covenant between me and you, and will multiply you exceedingly. . . . I will make nations of you, and kings shall come from you. And I will establish my covenant between me and you and your descendants after you. Also I give to you and your descendants after you the land in which you are a stranger, all the land of Canaan, as an everlasting possession; and I will be their God."   Genesis 17:1-8

Then Pharaoh spoke to Joseph, saying, "Your father and brothers dwell in the best of the land; let them dwell in the land of Goshen. . . . So Israel dwelt in the land of Egypt, in the country of Goshen; and they had possessions there and grew and multiplied exceedingly.   Genesis 47:5, 6, 27

And Joseph died, all his brothers and all that generation. . . . Now there arose a new king over Egypt, who did not know Joseph. And he said, "Look, the people of the children of Israel are mightier than we.". . . Therefore they set taskmasters over them to afflict them with their burdens. . . . So the Egyptians made the children of Israel serve with rigor. And they made their lives bitter with hard bondage.   Exodus 1:6-14

Now Moses kept the flock of Jethro his father-in-law, the priest of Midian. . . . And the Angel of the Lord appeared to him in a flame of fire from the midst of a bush. So he looked, and behold, the bush burned with fire, but the bush was not consumed. . . . God called to him from the midst of the bush and said, "Moses, Moses . . . I have surely seen the oppression of my people who are in Egypt. . . . Come now, therefore, and I will send you to Pharaoh that you may bring my people, the children of Israel, out of Egypt."   Exodus 3:1-10

CHAPTER ONE

Spiritual Bondage

Egypt

The freedom that goes with self-centeredness and materialism, and
their accompanying wants, is anything but freedom; it is utter slavery.

Arcana Coelestia 2884

Childhood Dreams

From the obscurity of the womb to the dawn of human consciousness, the Divine brings every person into the world. He
breaths into each tiny child's nostrils the breath of life, and that
child becomes a living human being. God then calls to the core
spirit within each human being to set out on a journey to find
wholeness and spirituality. All people can and will become gen-
uinely happy, spiritually aware, and healthy, if they take this journey. Even as the first words of God are spoken to Abram in the
beginning of the history of a nation, so the Divine speaks spiritually to each one of us: "Get out of your country . . . to a land that
I will show you. I will make you a great nation; I will bless you"
(Gen. 12:1-2).

This covenant between God and Abram is symbolic of the
covenant the Divine makes with you and me. From the very beginning God urges every person to rise from the inertia of self-centeredness and a preoccupation with the material world alone, to
move forward in a search for a new land and a new way. When a
person moves forward to find wholeness and spirituality, an inner
voice of the Divine begins to lead the way. The Divine will guide
and lead through a series of experiences, tests, and adventures,

3

toward a life that can truly be called blessed. In fact, the blessings from the Divine increase and never cease. As countless as the stars of the heavens, so will the number of those blessings be. According to the inner story of the Israelites' travel to a promised land, this new and happy life is our destiny. It is our promised land.

But that is the end in view, the goal, the final purpose. There is a journey that one must take to begin to understand that end. There is much to be learned in order to achieve that goal and realize that purpose. So the journey begins in childhood, in that dreamlike world of wonder and awe, in a world not too dissimilar from that of the biblical patriarchs Abraham, Isaac, and Jacob.

The patriarchs' stories in the book of Genesis have a childlike quality to them. As the reader follows the leaders through their lives' journeys, one cannot help but be struck by the dreamlike quality of their consciousness. The innocence, the simplicity, the childlike characteristics that these men and their families embody cause the reader to wonder and to yearn for his or her uncomplicated childhood.

Those first stories of the patriarchs are reminiscent of a childhood fantasy. Jacob rests with his head on a smooth rock in the middle of nowhere, dreaming of angels. Abraham and Sarah receive unexpected guests for dinner in the wilderness, none other than God himself, with two of his holy angels. Sarah giggles like a six-year-old when she learns she will conceive in her old age. The reader of these stories can sense the innocence of a simple kind of love as Isaac's servant searches to find him a wife and as Isaac is comforted by his new bride.

This biblical imagery conjures up childlike images, feelings, and emotive responses for good reason. The story of the book of Genesis, from Abram's call all the way to the children of Israel settling in Egypt, can be symbolic of the spiritual development we experienced as children. These first innocent, dreamlike years of this nation represent the first innocent, dreamlike years of you and me. Abraham, Isaac, and Jacob wander here and there so guilelessly through a land flowing with milk and honey. They embark on a new adventure each day, playing in the woods and fields, talking to angels, picking the fruit from every tree. And spiritually, you and I, as children, did the same thing.

Like these biblical characters, I remember well wandering in an inner paradisal state, in a land that flowed with wonder and delight. Like most children, I embarked on adventures with my friends, played, talked to angels, and ran from demons. We picked the good fruit from every tree. In fact, we had an apple orchard just across the road from our house that we raided periodically for its fruits. We built forts and camped for a time in one spot, only to pick up and move to a new location when the spirit called. We often sat and stared into the open sky and listened to the voice of nature all around. We also felt the pain of reality and the hurt that comes with the vulnerability of being a child. But because we didn't know any better, we still felt one with the world, accepted what came, were not afraid to trust, to hope, to give, and to grow. Childhood was a time of innocence and peace, a time when God could be with us because we hadn't learned yet to doubt.

Before the children of Israel ever found themselves in Egypt, they sojourned in the promised land of Canaan. They were a small group of wanderers, surrounded by many different nations and people. But they spent a peaceful and productive time under God's care and protection. Symbolically, in regard to our spiritual growth, Canaan represents the enchanted, innocent state of spiritual plenty in childhood. We are born there, into a type of innocence inherent in infancy and childhood. It is a type of spirituality, but not one that we have freely developed and can call our own. Just as the patriarchs were merely sojourning in Canaan, the spiritual land we inhabited as children was not ours. The fruit we picked as children was not our own fruit from our own orchards. Childhood innocence and its spirituality were gifts freely provided by the Divine, as we freely wandered here and there, playing, learning, growing, and accepting what this mystical paradise had to offer.

God gives people this first state of relative bliss to enjoy while they are young. In this way God can implant within every person memories of a richly blessed life. In childhood, the Divine instills memories of love, comfort and warmth, memories of wonder, of being one with the world, of the fruits of innocence and the blessedness of peace. The Divine implants these memories deep within human consciousness so that later, when people have grown, they will recall and long to return to that state, to begin to search for the wholeness and spirituality of the child within. As adults, with memories of this childhood innocence, people begin to seek a more spiritual and fulfilling life. This search will spark childhood feelings of absolute innocence, goodness, and peace. The adult longs for the child within, to return to this state, struggle for it, and even fight to reclaim it. But in the beginning, it is only a dream of childhood.

The Journey to Egypt

After years in Canaan, the children of Israel moved to Egypt because famine had swept the land. At their brother Joseph's request, they left their simple state of existence for a more advanced life in Egypt. This too is representative of people's early spiritual journey.

As children mature, they begin to want to make their own decisions. As they outgrow childhood, they begin to explore new areas and search for a way of life they can choose for themselves and call their own. They abandon their childhood bliss to explore new levels of awareness. That simple life in which everything spiritual seemed to be handed to them no longer suffices. The simple world doesn't seem that exciting anymore. It grows dry and pleasureless. Young men or women naturally begin to hunger for new and exciting challenges. They grow up and out of Canaan and head off to a new life of adventure, in a search for knowledge and understanding. Like the children of Israel who finally moved from Canaan and settled in Egypt, teenagers leave the comforts of an uncomplicated childhood for some excitement, action, new knowledge and under-standing. As they grow up, they finally move out of the uncompli-cated, sleepy life of Canaan to the fast-paced, culturally advanced, sophisticated world of Egypt.

You can imagine what Egypt represented to the sons of Israel and their families as they entered this new world for the first time. The sons of Israel were shepherds. They were tutored by their parents in rudimentary ways of knowledge. Their parents taught them simple concepts and instructions such as how to lead the flock out of the path of an oncoming bear or what to do if they lose a sheep out of the fold. No doubt, the Israelites's predominant architectural sight was their own tent. They glimpsed a few small cities or towns here and there; but all in all, the sons of Israel were babes in the simple life. Therefore, every facet of Egypt must have astonished them. The architecture alone far surpassed anything they had ever experienced. The system of government, commerce, industry, and agriculture must have seemed overwhelming. The scientific development in all these industries, as well as the sophis-ticated concepts of religion and philosophy must have seemed wondrous. To them, Egypt represented the pinnacle of human accomplishment. Egypt was science, intelligence, and human inge-nuity at its best.

Egypt can represent in spiritual and human development just about the same experience it represented to the Israelites. Egypt symbolizes a new way of perceiving the world. Moving from a foggy focus on spirituality, the young adolescent begins to turn eyes and ears to the external world. The focus turns to secular knowl-edge, science, human intelligence, and ingenuity. The Israelites' entrance into Egypt is symbolic of the entrance into adolescence when a new conceptual world emerges. The possibilities of life seem endless, enticing, and greater than the young person could have ever imagined as a child. A new world of learning and doing opens up; young adults begin to see what they can accomplish as competent human beings, if they use their potential. They begin to discover the ways of the world, to trust in their own intelligence and in what they learn from the external world around them.

In my years as a teacher and youth pastor, I have watched this ability to reason blossom inside the teenagers I taught. Initially their reason tends to be two-dimensional—right and wrong, black and white. But they do strive for what is fair, and most grow into a balanced adult outlook. Adolescents' ability to learn and grasp concepts is phenomenal, when the subject interests them. And often adolescents will ask the philosophical questions that adults are afraid to ask—questions about life-and-death issues, sexual issues, social issues, issues that parents would almost prefer not to talk about. They are willing to take risks in order to understand the world. They want to understand life. They want to succeed. Like the Egyptians, they have an extreme thirst for knowledge in all areas, but especially in the areas that will help them thrive in their worldly life, to build their personal empire, to achieve happiness and success.

On the other hand, along with its centers of learning, Egypt had its centers of corruption. The teen years are also a time of sensuality and excess. The adolescent world fast becomes a sensual world, where teenagers explore every sight and sound, taste, smell and touch. We may remember as teenagers how we overloaded our senses. Some of us lived a life of extremes. Our eyes gobbled up hour after hour of television. Our ears indulged in the loudest possible decibels of rock music. We stuffed pizza and popcorn into our mouths and washed it all down with a variety of sugared soft drinks. We splashed on the cologne, applied makeup and gel, whatever it would take to attract the opposite sex and to gain the acceptance of our peers. We explored the sense of touch and discovered our own sexuality and sexual expression. And this is just part of growing up. In many cases, our teen years also became times of sensual abuse—some of us experimented with drugs, alcohol, and unrestrained sexual practices. As teens we pushed all the limits. Like the Egyptians, we felt immortal.

I remember, for instance, on my sixteenth birthday taking my father's car for a ride that evening over a gravel road that wound perilously through a dense forest. The four passengers in my car screamed wildly as I was able to hit sixty and still make the turns through the trees. I remember well the car and driver I was racing just behind me. His name was Jamie, and he challenged me, "the birthday boy," to win my first race. I don't know if I felt invincible taking those turns at such a speed. I remember thinking for a brief moment how unpleasant it would be to die on my birthday. I think that one brief thought was enough to slow me down even for a moment and let Jamie pass. As he went by, he waved his arms out the window in a celebration of victory and with gestures of disgust toward my show of cowardice. I didn't think much about what it all meant then. It was one race of many, and not the last stupid act as an adolescent. But months later I did stop to think and, for a brief moment, felt the sense of the immortality of youth fade as Jamie's sister broke the news to a group of us that Jamie had been killed in a race in a nearby town not too far from our encounter. He had won the race and stuck his upper body out the car window in a show of victory and defiance. He lost control of the car and fell to the roadway. He was killed instantly.

This is a sad story but not a new story. Teenagers sometimes do stupid things and sometimes they get killed. But it is noteworthy to mention that within a few weeks most of us were racing again. This new world of what seemed to be unlimited power and unlimited possibilities was, in some ways, too much for us. While learning much about the world in this time of Egypt, humility and self-control were two traits that had not yet been learned or developed. There were other seemingly more important things to learn about, like getting to know the opposite sex, having a good time, and impressing our peers.

As life moves forward, problems begin to emerge. With the children of Israel problems began to develop years after they had settled in the land of Egypt. They should not have settled there long term. They could have stayed and learned from the Egyptians, fed themselves during the famine, been grateful guests, and then left. After the famine was over, they could have opted to leave Egypt; instead they opted to stay. The same is true in human spiritual development. People need the knowledge and sensual experience they discover as teenagers in order to learn how to live in the world as adults. Almost everyone experiences a period of development when the focus on life is mostly sensual, a time when we believe only what our senses tell us. But at some point each person must emerge from this state and pursue higher and more noble causes. For some, this transition seems to come naturally, and with little pain. Others never seem to grow up and out of their sense-oriented state of existence.

I remember counseling one man, whom I will call Doug, for drug and alcohol abuse. Actually, Doug came to me for marital counseling; but it turned out, as it often does, that addiction was the core problem. He was thirty-nine years old but acted like a sophomore in high school. In every facet of his life Doug thought and behaved like a fifteen-year-old—in his jokes, his attitude toward friends, authority figures, and his spouse. Doug and his wife were in the thickest codependent relationship I had ever seen. The relationship revolved around their addictions. When he finally was confronted with the issue of addiction, Doug stubbornly refused to deal with his problem. He said, "My wife and I are just a couple of kids who don't want to grow up. Is there anything wrong with that? Why should we grow up?" Doug eventually revealed that they had been getting stoned and drunk virtually every night of the week for the past sixteen years! They had never grown up; therefore, their relationship remained stilted and spiritually phlegmatic. It was a wonder they were still together at all, or in any semblance of physical health!

Somewhat like the arrested development of Doug and his wife, the Israelites too failed to grow into complete national and spiritual maturity while in Egypt. Historically, they stayed so long in Egypt that they virtually lost their identity as a people and lost sight of their destiny. In fact, they stayed so long that they eventually forgot about their God. They forgot about the land that God had promised them, they forgot about the simple life, having been swallowed up by Egypt. Spiritually, this becomes our problem as well. We can become swallowed up by "Egypt"—by materialism and sensuality. We focus in on this natural, earthly world. We forget about God, spirituality, and religion. The magic world of the Divine, and our childhood memories of a heavenly peace and joy fade away, and we become pagans of the corporate world. But this is only the beginning of our problems. Like the Israelites, as time passes, we wake up in a world very different from the one we used to know. When we remain in Egypt, we find ourselves in spiritual bondage.

Slaves

One day the children of Israel awakened to a world beyond their control and heading toward destruction. They had become strangers in a foreign land. They had become slaves under taskmasters assigned to work them into oblivion. They found themselves ruled by a tyrant, a new pharaoh who acted as if he were a god, by attempting to squash any person, people, or even nation that might threaten to disrupt his supreme authority and power. Many had come to live in fear and anxiety under this tyrant, who had even gone so far as to order that the newborn Israelite sons be immediately killed after birth. This madman of a king had commanded it to be so, for no reason at all, except to maintain his total control.

Not too long ago life in Egypt had been exciting and fun, and the children of Israel had found plenty of food to eat. They still had plenty of food, but this fact wasn't much consolation. When Joseph, who had invited them to Egypt, died, the hospitality of the Egyptians soon ended. Instead of being served, they became servants. Instead of being guests, they became grunts for the Egyptian taskmasters. This situation was mostly the fault of the new pharaoh who rose to power and who did not respect Joseph and the children of Israel. This pharaoh was demented from his lust for power. He had clandestine plans to wipe out the Israelites as a nation and had begun to execute his plans when he feared that they would threaten his power seat.

Slowly the chains of bondage tightened around the lives of the Israelites. Their already impossible load of work increased brick by brick each day. Rumors spread rapidly among the Israelites that pharaoh was after their children as well. There was such confusion. Some cried and cried over their plight, over their children, over their lives. Others took the best precautions they could and waited for the end. Still, others didn't comprehend their situation. They simply did what they were told. At least they had a roof over their heads and plenty of food to eat. That was all they knew. Who could blame them? What other choice did they have?

What a trap these Israelites found themselves in! Who doesn't sympathize with them as we read their story? On a spiritual level, you and I can identify with the plight of these people. We can feel their distress, the burdens, the insanity and confusion, the sense of hopelessness. It's all there, the human condition, described in the history of a people. As we come into adult life, most of us recognize this state of bondage. We have been there, perhaps we are still there, struggling for existence in this foreign land we call adult life. We have experienced this sense of inner bondage, symbolically, metaphorically, in our spiritual lives.

Perhaps the age is eighteen years old, perhaps twenty-two, maybe forty. But one day many people wake up and realize that they are not among friends any more. Like the Israelite slaves in Egypt, they have unwittingly become servants of their own egos and destructive tendencies. They begin to feel like prisoners in a superficial, worldly life apart from any type of spirituality. They can feel empty, alone, isolated from the rest of humanity, trapped in a private, ego-bound world.

The pharaoh they find ruling over them is the unrestrained ego and its pride. Pharaoh symbolizes the inflated ego, which takes power within and begins to reign like a tyrant. He thinks he knows everything and can control just about anything. He can become full of conceit, believing he has all power.

This new pharaoh is dangerous because he recognizes only his own prideful intelligence and what his senses tell him. This mind-set inevitably leads to hurt and pain. But this inner dictator is also demented, unleashing taskmasters within. The taskmasters pharaoh assigns are destructive tendencies, fears, and character defects, which can run a person ragged. A person can end up doing things that the more noble self would never have chosen to do. Some become driven by pride, or fear, or lust; some work to fulfill empty dreams or build useless monuments to manufactured gods. Eventually, even the most important treasures come into danger. What one might call our "spiritual children," the good things we have produced, nurtured and loved, become threatened by the inflated ego and its destructive tendencies.

You can, if you choose, recognize this bondage within you. At times, if you pay attention, you can sense an inner dictator at work. Perhaps, when in a dispute with your spouse or a co-worker, you sense it. The ego so easily flares up and becomes ready to attack. You may find you cannot control it, and it may cause you to burst out in anger and words of condemnation. You may sense this inner tyrant when you feel yourself becoming jealous over people or possessions you wish you had. Deep within, this dark force dictates commands that lead to manipulation, control, and selfishness.

Fears can also be merciless taskmasters. They can lord it over us and even cause us to act irrationally at times. Fear of rejection stops many from getting to know others intimately. Fear of the loss of control pushes some to dominate others. Fear of failure causes some to work too hard, or not at all. Fear of the harsh reality of life causes some to drink excessively or to use drugs. I know, for me, one taskmaster is the fear of failure, another is the fear of not being liked, still another is the inner taskmaster that tells me that, if I don't keep myself busy at all times, I should feel guilty for not making myself useful. These are some of mine. I am sure you know your own taskmasters and what they tell you.

I once knew a man who experienced a phase in his life when his fear of failure became such a ruthless taskmaster that he could not work. He had become so frightened that he would not meet the boss's standards that eventually, instead of working harder, becoming more efficient, and producing more, he began to produce less and less. His fears beat him so hard each day that he became weak and unable to perform tasks that co-workers could perform with ease. The final straw came when a supervisor was scheduled to observe his work. He couldn't bear that. In fact, the very day this observation was to begin, he quit his job to look for another. His personal taskmaster had broken his back.

Sometimes the taskmasters that control people are quite evident. They are well-known, though not well liked. Some people, like the children of Israel, are forced to build useless monuments out of bricks. The bricks are lies they tell themselves that they stack on top of one another, building up a false image of self and their own sense of importance. People can work hard for what amounts to practically no real or long-lasting benefit, piling one lie on top of the other, building monuments to human folly, but claiming they mean so much more.

For instance, the compulsive hunger for corporate success can be quite a taskmaster to work under. It has destroyed many lives. A young man (or woman) who is driven to make as much money as possible and acquire as much power as possible builds wonderfully impressive but wonderfully useless monuments to himself. He may have money, but no true friends or perhaps no real family anymore to spend it with. He may have the expensive toys, the sports car, the cottage at the beach, the boat, but no one to share them with. This is because he has—if not physically, then emotionally—left everyone else behind to achieve his "success." His taskmasters within have convinced him to sacrifice family, friendships, and love for the trappings of success. He can buy friendships, but they, like his possessions, will not fulfill him because they are superficial. These possessions, and even the "friends," make wonderful trophies testifying to the remarkable achievements of a driven and inflated ego, but deep inside they seem so empty to him. Like the pharaoh's tombs, they are empty palaces with the pretense of life within them. But they are as dead as an Egyptian mummy!

Another taskmaster that many of us know all too well is that of addiction. The person who slaves under this master is often forced to work overtime to get the job done. But it never works out right; the monuments keep tumbling. The taskmaster whips hard and often. The slave runs back for more bricks, leaving the old mess behind, sweating to make everything come out right, working to cover over mistakes. The slave thirsts for a cool drink that never comes, forever needing the fix that he or she must have at all costs. If the taskmaster says "Lie," the addicted slave will do so. If it means compromising her morals, she does not refuse. He will betray friends. She will leave her children. He will lie and cheat. She will manipulate and cajole. He will cover up. She will cover up. That's the way people work in this house of bondage called addiction.

Finally, for some of us, even the beautiful things we love are threatened. Our spiritual children, the good things we have brought forth and nurtured in life, begin to suffer under the rule of our inflated ego. Perhaps these spiritual children are relationships that begin to wither and die. Sometimes the inner dictator is more interested in power than in relationships, in sex rather than love, in the euphoria of chemical escape rather than the simple pleasure of care and responsibility over family or job or even self. So the ego carelessly orders that we neglect the good things to achieve those selfish compulsions. Perhaps these children who are in danger of being destroyed are simply the pleasant feelings we enjoy from time to time. For instance, our sense of peace and well-being, once valued, may seem to disappear overnight. We find ourselves waking alone, bereaved of a sense of tranquility, nervous and anxious about the future. The more precious parts of our character are threatened with destruction because the ego doesn't know when to quit, because our fears can run us ragged, because compulsions can cause us to neglect, even to harm what we love the most.

This dismal picture rings true for many people. But I realize that some do not readily sense these bonds of Egypt. People go through this stage of life at different intervals, with varying degrees of awareness. Some people pass through Egypt very quickly and apparently without much pain. Some struggle greatly to escape the force of their destructive tendencies and addictions. Some never get out of Egypt. And there are also those who are, indeed, slaves to their own hidden and destructive dictators, but don't even know it. They are represented by those Israelites who refused to recognize what was happening to them. Denial is not a new phenomenon. Regardless, I believe everyone who wishes to have a truly happy life must, at some time, recognize that he or she is in a type of bondage and must make a conscious effort to escape, with God's help, and to head off toward a promised land.

A Leader for Israel

God did not abandon Israel to remain forever in Egypt under such terrible conditions. He raised up a leader to confront pharaoh and take his people out of this land toward a new land of freedom and prosperity. The Divine, or God as we understand him, does not abandon us either. He raises up such a leader within us and within our own consciousness, a leader who also faces the interior pharaoh, a leader who will show us the way to a new and prosperous life. That leader is Moses.

Moses symbolizes the active role of truth within us, what some call the Word and others the Logos. Moses represents the laws of life and revelation. If you think about it, it is truth that will pull any individual out of the slavery of egotism and selfishness. Truth about self, about life, about God, and about the right way will lead the person out of bondage to a new freedom, even as it says in the Gospels, "You shall know the truth, and the truth will make you free" (John 8:32).

That Moses represents the law is not a new concept. The Jews throughout the centuries commonly referred to the Old Testament as "Moses and the prophets" or "the law and the prophets." The first five books of the Old Testament are called "the books of Moses." And when Jesus was transfigured on the mount in front of Peter, James, and John, there appeared with him Moses and Elijah (Matt. 17:3). Moses' presence represented the law and Elijah's the prophets; and, for Christians, Jesus' presence with these revered figures was a sign that his word was to be equal to their word.

In adult life, even as individuals suffer from an inner sense of slavery and bondage, something else has been blossoming simultaneously within, the truth that will set us free. Moses, representing the law, symbolizes the simple truth acquired as children. It may exist in the form of the lessons we learned in Sunday school, the Ten Commandments, the Golden Rule, the basic rules of life. It is neither very developed nor profound. You may recall from Exodus 4:10 that even Moses needed Aaron, his brother, to speak for him in public because he was "slow of speech." Nevertheless, Moses would serve to lead the people out of Egypt and to their rightful home. So too, the truth we know is rudimentary, perhaps it even stutters within us, but it will serve us and lead us to our rightful spiritual home.

When we were infants, this truth was hidden in the bulrushes of our inner memories, protected from the ego and its taskmasters. As we grew, this truth represented by Moses was kept and preserved by none other than pharaoh's daughter herself right under her father's nose. She saw the child floating in the basket in the bulrushes, took him up, fell in love with him, and decided to take him home and have him raised as part of the family. She unknowingly selected Moses' own mother to nurse the child while he was a babe.

Even pharaoh's daughter has a representation. She is the off-spring of our ego, symbolizing a natural love that springs from the pride of our own intellect—a love for learning. Pharaoh's daughter, representing within us a natural love for learning, sees this baby Moses, the divine law, and thinks it's cute! Yes, cute. She holds onto it and cares for it until it can stand up for itself in adult age. Even as people grow and become secular, or nonreligious, they still tend to respect those childhood truths. Like pharaoh's daughter, they see something innocent and special about these tender truths and want to nurture and protect them. For instance, though individuals may not practice a certain religion anymore, they may still celebrate their former faith's customs. A non-practicing Christian may still celebrate Christmas and Easter. Many still choose to marry in a church, not necessarily because they continue to believe what the church teaches, but because in childhood these traditions seemed so special. Many of us retain the customs, images, and truths for which we hold a special feeling. That's pharaoh's daughter raising Moses.

As the truth that Moses represents grows within us, its force increases. The power of truth, especially early in life, can be unrestrained and harsh. For instance, in the beginning of our spiritual growth, our judgment is often not tempered with mercy. We see something we know is true and we use it to condemn, not only others but ourselves as well. When we recall certain moral codes about forgiveness, love, and morality, we recognize that we are not adhering to those codes. So we may punish ourselves or make ourselves feel excessively guilty. We condemn ourselves on account of our shortcomings. This is represented by Moses killing an Egyptian.

The adult Moses is walking along the city streets when he sees an Egyptian beating an Israelite. He doesn't just stop the Egyptian; he hauls off and kills him. So too, there may come a time when the truth is harsh and destructive within us. Its power awes us as it knocks down and obliterates, for instance, false ideas that had

oppressed us for so long; but we are afraid of this truth. It is so judg-
mental and condemning. It provokes guilt. Moses, for instance,
walks into the street the next day and everyone stares at him. He
tries to stop two Israelites from fighting, and one turns to him and
asks, "Are you going to kill me too?" (Exodus 2:14). Moses sees that
everybody knows. Everybody's apprehensive. Everybody's talking. Moses realizes he had better go into hiding.

Moses kills the Egyptian, wonders why he cared so much or got
so involved in the Israelite people's plight to begin with, packs his
bags and heads off to the mountains for the simple life, away from
these people and their plight. When we see the conflict between
what we have learned in childhood, and the slavery and pain of our
present life, we too may pack up and try to run away from it.

Moses escapes to the mountains of Midian to avoid the madness.
He becomes a shepherd, caring for the sheep, studying by the well,
reflecting under the trees, and gazing off into the horizon from atop
the mountains. He finds a wife there, the daughter of Jethro. Life
seems quite good. Perhaps he feels a bit guilty about the poor
Israelites he left back in Egypt, but this modest life sure beats the
Egyptian madness. He promises himself that he'll never return to
face that mess.

Can we relate to this attitude? How many of us dropped everything and metaphorically headed off to the mountains at one time
or another? If we didn't actually do it after college or high school,
we certainly wanted to. It's human nature. We decide not to deal
with the dilemma we are now facing in adult life, the dilemma
between good and evil, right and wrong, the moral and immoral,
but rather to escape from it. We may feel we don't have to play the
game. We don't have to respond to pharaoh or Egypt or Israel. We
believe we can run away, get married, have some kids, feed sheep,
work, read, reflect, and live happily ever after. But life isn't that
simple, and our problems don't go away.

The truth within can become dormant. Moses does run and hide.
And we sometimes run away and hide from our problems. But no

matter how far away the inner Moses runs, he hears the yell of the Egyptian taskmasters, the crack of the whips, and the cry of his fellow countrymen. We may deny the pain but it is still there. We cannot forget it. It is real, and it will not go away until we face it.

One day as Moses walks through the mountains tending his flocks, he notices a burning bush in front of him—a strange sight indeed, but stranger than this is the fact that, although the bush is burning, it is not being consumed. A different kind of fire is burning in this bush. Then God speaks, "Moses, Moses, . . . I am the God of Abraham, the God of Isaac, and the God of Jacob. . . . I have surely seen the oppression of my people who are in Egypt, and have heard their cry because of their taskmasters, for I know their sorrows. So I have come down to deliver them out of the hand of the Egyptians, and to bring them up from that land to a good and large land, to a land flowing with milk and honey. . . . Come now, therefore, and I will send you to Pharaoh, that you may bring my people, the children of Israel, out of Egypt" (Exodus 3:4-10).

One day as we walk through a similar mountain path, we are struck by the perception that we are not alone. A voice deep inside calls to us. It may come in the form of an insight, or just a little burning sense of hope, of love. That fire that does not consume is love, or rather, *Love*. It is love itself, the God of our childhood calling to us, the God of Abraham, Isaac, and Jacob. We come upon a flame of insight, a hope, a faint certainty that someone other than ourselves has witnessed our suffering. We perceive that, indeed, someone other than ourselves does love and care for us and has not forgotten us. We begin to feel that maybe, just maybe, we can be free. God commands us from the bush to go back. He commands Moses, the truth we do know about life, to go back and face that monster of an ego. Face him. Tell him the truth, that it's over, that there is a God and it isn't pharaoh. And that this God, a power greater than any earthly king, army, or empire, will bring his people out from under pharaoh's destructive control. Moses is commanded to go back to pharaoh and say, "Thus says the Lord God of Israel: Let my people go" (Exodus 5:1).

Exercises

1. On a piece of paper write down three childhood experiences that remain special. What lessons have these experiences taught you? How do they point to a better way of life?

2. What are the taskmasters in your life? Can you list them? Which habits or thought patterns prevent happiness in your life? Pick one of these habits and decide not to do it for one day. Can you feel its power? How can you adjust your life to live without it every day?

3. Where do you find direction for your life? This week, find a Bible, or other spiritual material, and begin to read portions of it each day. Do new thoughts begin to lead you?

Moses and Aaron went in and told Pharaoh, "Thus says the Lord God of Israel: 'Let my people go.' . . . And Pharaoh said, "Who is the Lord, that I should obey his voice to let Israel go? I do not know the Lord, nor will I let Israel go." Exodus 5:1-2

And Aaron cast down his rod before Pharaoh and before his servants, and it became a serpent. But Pharaoh also called the wise men and the sorcerers . . . and they also did in like manner with their enchantments. For every man threw down his rod, and they became serpents. Exodus 7:10-12

And the Lord said to Moses, "I will bring yet one more plague on Pharaoh and on Egypt. Afterward he will let you go from here. . . . About midnight I will go out into the midst of Egypt; and all the firstborn in the land of Egypt shall die. . . . Then there shall be a great cry throughout all the land of Egypt, such as was not like it before, nor shall be like it again. Exodus 11:1, 4-6

Then it came to pass, when Pharaoh had let the people go, that . . . God led the people around by way of the wilderness of the Red Sea. And the children of Israel went up in orderly ranks out of the land of Egypt. Exodus 13:17, 18

The children of Israel lifted their eyes, and behold, the Egyptians marched after them. So they were very afraid. . . . The Lord said to Moses, ". . . lift up your rod, and stretch out your hand over the sea and divide it. And the children of Israel shall go on dry ground through the midst of the sea.". . . Then Moses stretched out his hand over the sea; and the Lord caused the sea to go back, . . . and made the sea into dry land; and the waters were divided. So the children of Israel went into the midst of the sea on the dry ground. Exodus 14:10-22

CHAPTER TWO

Road to Recovery

Exodus

God does not tempt anyone. In times of temptation he is constantly rescuing the person from it . . . and he constantly has good as an end toward which he leads the person who is undergoing temptations.

Arcana Coelestia 2768

Signs and Wonders

Moses reluctantly accepted God's commission to return to Egypt to confront pharaoh and secure the freedom of the Israelites. God promised that Moses' brother, Aaron, would help him. Upon returning, Moses enlisted Aaron to speak for him in public, because Moses was "slow of speech." Together they began to gather the people and prepare them to confront pharaoh. The two of them then secured an appointment with the pharaoh, came before him, and demanded that he release the children of Israel.

God had instructed Moses and Aaron to carry a wooden rod, which, if pharaoh resisted them, they should cast down to the earth where it would become a snake. If that did not sway pharaoh, then Aaron was instructed to wave the rod over the Nile river and to strike the water, which would turn to blood. And if that still did not move the pharaoh to allow the Israelites to leave Egypt, then Aaron should wave the rod again, and frogs would come forth from the Nile and infest all of Egypt. These signs and wonders were intended to impress pharaoh and convince him to let the children of Israel go on their journey.

But pharaoh was not impressed. Why not? Because he called in his own magicians who were able to perform the same tricks. They too threw down their rods and produced snakes. They too changed the water into blood. They too drew forth frogs from the river. Imagine the laughter and ridicule. Why should pharaoh be impressed when his own magicians could perform every so-called "miracle" of the Israelite God?

How odd that God instructed Moses to perform miracles that the Egyptians could also perform! How cruel—it's almost a practical joke—that God led Moses and Aaron into a false sense of power and security, only to reveal that the miracles he had given them were no better than a magician's bag of tricks. God's actions do seem odd and cruel when one sees only a literal meaning. But when viewed as an allegory that reflects a person's spiritual development, God's actions begin to make sense. We see that God's first signs and wonders can indeed be duplicated by humans; and that, in the beginning, no matter what warning signs people may receive about their spiritual life, they are usually not impressed and certainly not ready to change.

I've said that Moses can represent the active truth within us, the law. Aaron, Moses' interpreter and spokesman, represents the understanding, or interpretation, of this truth. Pharaoh's being confronted by Moses and Aaron symbolizes a person's ego being confronted by the truth, or the best understanding the person has of it. The truth warns the ego that if it doesn't change, if it doesn't allow the wholesome instincts to emerge and seek a new way of life, troubled times lay ahead. The ego will set off a series of plagues in the person's life, and those plagues will progressively worsen.[1] Each person must break free from the pharaoh within and head off toward a new way of life.

---

1. In the biblical story, God brings the plagues; this is symbolic of the way we view God in times of trouble. We blame him for causing the plagues, but it only appears that God is the cause of our misfortune. Actually, we bring the plagues upon ourselves.

What does this mean on a practical level? It means that one day you and I begin to be confronted with the truth about our lives. The truth represented by Moses confronts the ego, perhaps warning us that if we continue to try to control every aspect of our world, we will self-destruct. Or the truth warns that we must stop manipulating if we want our marriage to last; or if we continue to use people, we will lose our friends. With some, the Moses within warns that their drug or alcohol consumption is out of control and that the plagues of addiction are about to begin, real plagues with devastating results. Moses' and Aaron's warnings to pharaoh symbolize the first warnings that, if the ego's dominance is not thwarted, dire consequences will be suffered.

As we have seen, the first sign given to pharaoh was that Aaron's wooden rod was cast down and turned into a snake. This sign has a specific spiritual meaning. This meaning may initially appear to have nothing to do with rods and snakes. But every time the rod image is repeated in this biblical story its spiritual meaning is confirmed. The wooden rod always represents the power of goodness. The wooden rod is not a very exalted or spiritual goodness. Unlike the truth represented by Moses, it is rudimentary, merely a stick in the hand; but it is strong enough to hold us up on our long journey and to protect us from evil along the way. Think of this rod as the basic good we know and hold in our life.

The wooden rod's becoming a snake represents a warning to the ego that, if it doesn't change its ways, even the rudimentary goodness that one enjoys will become corrupt. It will become snake-like—earthy, sensual, crawling on and lapping up the dust of the ground. In Egypt, a worldly life devoid of spirituality, the ego rules without any acknowledgment of a power greater than self. If a person remains in Egypt, then even those moments of love, peace, contentment, and happiness that are glimpsed from time to time can turn earthly, devoid of spiritual value. Without a conscious effort to work on marriage, for instance, love for the partner can degenerate into self-fulfillment and satisfaction, at the expense of our partner's happiness. Without a deliberate search for love and understanding, daily interactions with family and friends can turn empty and superficial. Without a new resolve to search for wholeness and spirituality, love for life can become a compulsion for the quick fix: the empty euphoria of drug and alcohol use, the sensual satisfaction of gluttony, the rush of sexual excitement, or perhaps, the high of dominating and controlling others. Without a search for spirituality, the little goodness we do enjoy in our lives can turn into snakes.

My own inner Moses has warned me at several significant times in my life. The first time the warning was strong, easy to remember and describe, because I really got the message. As a teenager I led my own gang of suburban kids. We would run wild in the middle of the night, stealing booze and even food from people's houses, getting drunk and feasting under the moon and stars until dawn. We once stole a roast beef from the table of an elderly woman after she had stepped out for a minute—one of our "finest" moments. After I was caught and arrested, I went to court and was put on probation, which was fair enough for an adolescent's first encounter with the law. But two days later I was caught breaking into a friend's empty house during the wee morning hours. (I merely wanted to borrow my friend's guitar. I didn't see any problem with that back then, which certainly shows the illusions under which I led my life.) No one reported this incident to the police, but I remember my parents' reaction clearly.

My parents didn't yell. In fact, their shock and desperation rendered them almost speechless. That was perhaps the loudest message they could have given me. The sound of my mother, crying out of desperation, and the sight of my father, his face blank with bewilderment and loss of hope, at once broke me down. I saw the effects of my behavior. Neither threats nor beatings nor sentencing turned me around. A vision of the pain I caused, and a perception that my parents' lives, as well as my own, were heading toward more and more pain, penetrated my consciousness. I didn't want to go downhill. I didn't want to end up in jail, or relocate in a home for juvenile delinquents. But mostly I didn't want to hurt my parents anymore. I saw how the good and the peace of mind that they had struggled for in their efforts to raise their children were being cast down and turned into a snake. And I was responsible for that. I decided to turn my life around, for myself and for them. And I did begin to change. Although I had many more plagues or challenges before me, that particular incident marked the beginning of my spiritual quest, when the inner Moses first summoned me to leave Egypt for a new way of life.

In the biblical story, after the rod became a snake, Aaron needed to offer pharaoh the second warning sign: he changed the waters of the Nile into blood. The Egyptians' only life source, the waters of the Nile, became contaminated. Aaron's warning illuminates a key interior meaning that emerges repeatedly in the Exodus story: the spiritual meaning of water.

In the Bible, water symbolizes truth. But while Moses represents the law aspect of the truth, water represents the living truth that can cleanse, heal, quench spiritual thirst, and give life. This symbolism becomes clear when we examine how "water" is used in the Bible. In John 4:10-14, we find Jesus saying to the woman by the well, "If you knew the gift of God and who it is who says to you, 'Give Me a drink,' you would have asked Him, and He would have given you living water. . . . Whoever drinks of the water that I shall give him will never thirst." In Revelation 21:6, we are promised that in the age to come, "I will give of the fountain of the water of life freely to him who thirsts." Both passages describe the living truth that the divine offers, truth that will revive and sustain us.

Other stories in the Bible also confirm the spiritual meaning of water. When Naaman, who suffers from leprosy, is told to bathe in the Jordan to be made whole, he does so, and his skin becomes as fresh as a child's. The water of the Jordan River, flowing as it does on the brink of the promised land, symbolizes the truth that brings about life-change. Naaman's washing in the Jordan symbolizes how we can use the truth to cleanse our outward actions, which will restore us to wholeness and heal the spiritual diseases that afflict us. Then we can make sense of what Isaiah told his people, "Wash yourselves, make yourselves clean, put away the evils of your doing. . . . Though your sins are like scarlet, they shall be as white as snow" (Isaiah 1:16-18). The blind man is told by Jesus to go and wash his eyes in the pool, the cripple waits for the water to be stirred to dip himself in to be healed, the children of Israel thirst for water in a dry land and are given drink. All of these represent the living truth that we can freely receive from our God, the truth that will refresh, enliven, sustain us, and help us grow.

When the Nile is turned into blood as a warning to pharaoh, it becomes putrid and undrinkable. The admonition Aaron gives pharaoh symbolizes that the truth we know, love, and live by will become false, polluted, and unhealthy if we do not change our ways and leave "Egypt" so that we may progress spiritually. In the Bible water represents truth; but when putrefied or used in a bad sense, it takes on the opposite meaning, falsity.

There isn't a pure truth within any heart or mind that can't be tainted by the influence of selfishness and egotism. Parents, for example, may believe they know how to raise their children correctly, but when the pharaoh within is in charge, discipline can take the form of scolding, berating, manipulation, and even physical abuse. The truth a parent knows about raising children can become perverted and tainted. For example, it may be true that discipline is essential, that firm, fair punishment is necessary from time to time. But if ruled by pharaoh, how easy it is to pollute that truth, so that use of discipline becomes abuse of discipline.

It may be a truth that an individual should stand up for what is right. But if pharaoh is in charge, full of conceit and jealous for power and attention, this water of truth can be made undrinkable too. Individuals, for example, can find themselves piously protecting the truth by exploiting the wrongs of others. They may gossip about co-workers, character-assassinate the boss, criticize in-laws behind their backs, and justify their actions to themselves and others by claiming that they must expose the truth to protect and inform the company, or the family, or the children. In fact, they may not care at all about these things. They just operate under the conscious or unconscious assumption that denigrating others exalts themselves. So they taint the truth while claiming to protect it. They end up turning the water into blood.

This applies to every truth we know. Human beings can deftly pervert the truth in a state of egotism, evil, or disorder. We can alter its living and pure state to something harmful and noxious. Moses and Aaron warn us that we will, indeed, begin to taint the truth if our pharaoh doesn't pay attention to them instead of his own magicians.

Now God's next warning, or plague, and the subsequent plagues represent more particular noxious spiritual problems. The frogs emerging from the putrid water can symbolize the thousands of croaking false reasons, the tainted thoughts that leap into our consciousness from the polluted waters of our minds. The frogs are said to have hopped into everything in Egypt: into the people's beds, ovens, kitchen plates and bowls. They were the third sign and warning. The plague of selfishness and human conceit won't stay in a polluted river. It will hop into other aspects of one's life and spoil them.

This sounds almost comical, doesn't it? It is comical, in a sense, especially when we see pharaoh and his magicians do the same thing. Pharaoh watches each of these first three signs and warnings, turns to his magicians, and says, "Hit it, boys!" And they produce the same plagues. They too can turn their rods into snakes. Big deal! Never mind that Aaron's snake eats theirs! They can always make new ones. And water to blood? They learned that trick way back in Sorcery 101! Never mind that they can't drink the water for seven days. They had plenty of Israelite slaves to dig a few wells elsewhere for a while. And frogs? Easier than pulling a rabbit out of a hat. So what if they can't get rid of them once they produce them? Nobody's perfect! But boy, oh boy, what a joke this Moses and Aaron have turned out to be!

What does it mean in our spiritual lives that pharaoh and his henchmen can produce the same results as Moses and Aaron? It means that the puffed-up ego can observe these warnings and prove with human reasoning that they are just tricks. God's warnings don't impress our ego because it can prove anything it chooses. Humans have the capability of rationalizing excuses for anything they choose. The ego-dominated intellect can make any statement appear true and any statement appear false.

For instance, we may note a warning from our conscience that we are becoming too sensual and losing our spirituality, but our ego doesn't really care. What's wrong with a little fun? The ego can create that same picture of the sensual life in our imagination and make it look like fun, not something to be concerned about. Of course, Aaron's snake eats pharaoh's, showing us that God's truth about our condition is real and the ego's "truth" an illusion, but the ego doesn't pay attention to that. We can sense the inner warning that whatever truth we know is in danger of being turned to blood, but again, the ego is not impressed. Our ego-dominated intellect can picture that scenario in our own minds and tell us that anything can have good or bad consequences. We repeat to ourselves the refrain that is heard a lot nowadays, "Truth is relative." We can imagine noxious things crawling into our lives, but the ego tells us "Hey, they're only cute little frogs! They're just harmless thoughts. They can't hurt us."

The human mind can prove anything. The ego has its magicians. It can prove that up is down, black is white, in is out; and it's no sweat to prove that good is evil and evil is good, or that neither is anything. The ego has its magicians. So much for signs and wonders.

Sliding toward the Bottom

The first signs and plagues didn't devastate the Egyptians. One snake, one river of blood, one temporary frog infestation—these were manageable. Besides, the magicians were competent, repeatedly proving that Moses and Aaron's warnings were mere tricks.

Now it is true that pharaoh's magicians could not reverse the plagues they created. Only Moses, and the God of Moses, had that power, which symbolizes the fact that the ego is ultimately out of our control. It can create disorder but can't summon the means to restore order. The ego is out of control without a higher power to guide it. Like pharaoh and his magicians, the ego creates the illusion that it is in control, but it is powerless over the plagues it starts and the plagues that follow.

The magicians duplicated the first plagues for pharaoh, but the following plagues had the magicians worried. They couldn't copy them anymore. As the plagues progressively worsened, the magicians started to warn pharaoh that this couldn't be a trick; this was, indeed, "the finger of God" (Exodus 8:19). When our spiritual life begins to deteriorate, alarms ring in our head, to warn our ego that danger exists, but the ego thinks it knows better. Pharaoh's heart was hardened. He couldn't turn back. He was locked in a power struggle to the end. He would squeeze those Israelites into submission! After all, he was pharaoh, the supreme ruler, both king and lord. As he tried to hold on with his power, each new plague made Egyptian life more and more bleak, and pharaoh's own life was progressively becoming more unmanageable and unbearable.

The plagues that followed the first three embody specific meanings as well. Each plague represents a spiritual condition we bring upon ourselves. Each illustrates a progression toward increasingly more tragic states of disorder, pain, and unmanageableness. We see pharaoh getting battered by each plague, saying that enough is enough. But when each plague subsides, he changes his mind until the next plague compounds his problems. That's our ego refusing to give up, rationalizing, denying, until our spiritual situation deteriorates and weakens to the breaking point.

Upon examination, the first plagues are merely bothersome, a nuisance—frogs, lice (actually gnats from the ground), and the noisome fly. These represent the bothersome but not necessarily devastating plagues that come into our lives. These plagues symbolize base wants and desires, springing up like gnats out of the ground into our conscious minds, or noxious thoughts that buzz like flies through our minds to plague us. For instance, some people are distracted by sexual thoughts, like the man plagued with pornographic images, hoards of filthy jokes hopping into his mind, buzzing around his empty head aimlessly and disturbing its surroundings. For some, these gnats and flies symbolize thoughts of abandonment, of inadequacy, of futility, of being unlikable, of being hurt. These insects can symbolize our angry and jealous thoughts that tell us when others attain success it's not fair and that we deserve so much more than the competitors. Self-pity, morose musings, and depressing reflections may plague a person. As long as this first phase of plagues remains in our heads without affecting our outward lives, the plagues remain bearable. They may be a terrible nuisance, but we tolerate them.

Unfortunately, as long as our personal pharaoh retains power over our exit from Egypt, the plagues become increasingly intolerable. The livestock's becoming diseased symbolizes good feelings turned into sick feelings. Boils appearing on the skin symbolize character defects coming to the surface and marring our daily lives—they aren't just thoughts anymore. They appear in words and deeds that inflict pain on ourselves and others. Hail rains down from the sky destroying most of our crops; then come the locusts to finish off what is left—these represent how defects of character and false ideas rain down destruction into our daily lives. Our crops, the fruits we have cultivated, become damaged by unbridled defects. We can find ourselves damaging our lives and the lives we touch. Moreover, darkness descends and conquers all: the dense ignorance from the spiritual vacuum encompasses us. The darkness and gloom settle within our conscious minds.

But what punctuates this process again and again? Pharaoh, our own ego, says, "OK, OK, enough is enough. I want to change. I don't want these plagues anymore. I'm willing to let go, try a new way, give up the power seat." We pray when we're in a jam, "Please

God, take the problem away and I'll change. I'll start again. I'll turn over a new leaf." But when the pain is gone, so often too are the promises. Our pharaoh says, "Life wasn't so bad." He reminds us, "I'm still in control here, aren't I?" We go back to our old ways. Our old ways continue until finally the worst confronts us.

The worst doesn't have to happen in our outward lives. It can happen in our hearts. It can happen in the imagination alone, if we are lucky. But if the ego refuses to let go, eventually we experience the final plague: the death of our firstborn. In the biblical story, all of the Egyptians' firstborn children die, including pharaoh's son. You and I may experience a similar fate on a spiritual level. We may awake one day to the absence of what was once the most treasured part of our lives. We may see the shell that once was our life and our dreams, and we weep over its emptiness. Our hopes and dreams are dead. We stare into the emptiness, the darkness and the abyss, and like pharaoh who lost his child, we mourn our loss.

Strictly speaking, this death symbolizes the death of the ego's grandiose vision—the cherished belief that we can control it all. We suddenly find out we cannot. This "death" also symbolizes our sense of emptiness when we realize we are nothing without God. We might have to face the reality that we are not who we thought we were and that we never will be, which can be like a death, the death of a vision of self. We may wake up and notice an emptiness where our love for life or for others once dwelled. The emptiness and coldness can fill us with horror.

In some instances, this final plague can be more than a spiritual loss; for some people it can be real and substantial. Some find that burned bridges with their spouse have led to the death of their marriage. For some, stubbornness, egotism, laziness, or another character defect has run rampant for so long that they lose their job because of their behavior. Warnings sounded, and the plagues increased; but they ignored them until it was too late.

I must stress that we don't necessarily have to lose what is most valuable in our outward lives, or even in the inner lives of our heart,

to experience the final plague. Being open and honest with ourselves, we can experience this death in our imaginations alone. We
can imagine our destination before we arrive and turn away from
self-centeredness to God-centeredness, from the inevitability of
death to the promise of new life. Pharaoh can be broken and allow
us to move off toward the promised land without losing our spouse,
children, house, or job. In fact, most on this spiritual path don't
actually lose these things. But some do, and you and I can and will
lose our inward sense of life, happiness, and well-being, if we don't
heed the word of Moses. Pharaoh must listen or the plagues will
descend. Pharaoh must be broken, give up, and let go absolutely. It
is not until we submit to the divine will that we can escape our self-
inflicted plagues or bondage.

Drug and alcohol abuse provides an appropriate example of this
entire process. I believe that alcoholism and drug addiction are
not sins but sicknesses. Still, if this sickness is not treated, it causes
rampant evil in a person's life and the lives it touches. Alcohol and
drug addiction are dysfunctional, disorderly ways of living. They
hurt and kill not only the body but the spirit. Without a complete
and definite decision to move forward, out of the grasp of the disease, an alcoholic is doomed to face the plagues that the disease
inflicts.

How many alcoholics or drug addicts wake up in the morning
after a terrible binge and speak and act just like pharaoh? "OK, I've
had enough. I'm ready to try something new," they may say. How
many times has a person in this predicament pleaded with God,
pounding head, nausea, buzzing flies, sweat and all, "God, just get
me out of this and I'll turn over a new leaf." Like pharaoh, his or
her ego says, "God, please, remove this plague, and I'll do whatever you want."

What happens next? Exactly what happened with pharaoh.
Once the plague subsides the self-reliant human intelligence takes
over and says, "It wasn't so bad, was it?" Usually by that afternoon
the alcoholic, a new drink in hand, or the drug addict with his fix

doesn't even remember the plague from the night before. He refuses to allow his more noble self to be set free to search for wholeness. He spends another drunken and fearful night with the flies, locusts, dead animals, disease, and darkness. It is usually not until he loses what is most precious to him, represented by the firstborn of Egypt, that he finally says, "My God, enough is enough! I am ready to listen. Please free me from these plagues!"

This process can also be illustrated in the realm of codependency. A woman awakens to find herself in this house of bondage called codependency, trapped by her habit of blindly putting her partner's concerns before her own, caring for him no matter what he does to her, rescuing him from his own snares, bandaging his self-inflicted wound, while ignoring the wounds he has inflicted on her. She has tried to escape this relationship, or at least to change it, but she feels guilty and uncaring when she moves away from him. As the relationship progressively degenerates, she steels herself and says, "OK, I can't take it anymore! I've got to change this relationship." But then, her partner backs off for a few days, and the plagues seem to clear up for a while, until she forgets and pretends to herself that things were "never really that bad." This scenario repeats itself through times of bitterness and resentment to arguments, accusations, physical pain—all of which are the progressive plagues of codependency—until she finally experiences the death of something she really cares about. She loses her dignity perhaps, as she watches him gloat over other women, or her sense of justice, as he pushes her aside at every turn. She doesn't initiate any constructive action until she stares death right in the face.

The same is true with all the evils people suffer from in their personal lives— pride, greed, lust, anger, gluttony, envy, and laziness. They may toy with these. They get a certain delight out of them. The more they act on their destructive tendencies, the more they suffer from the plagues that lie hidden within them. They may repeat this until they have been hurt so badly, either inwardly or even outwardly in daily life, that they hit bottom. Something inside dies. They begin to feel broken, empty, and powerless. Hopefully, they finally give up and let a power greater than self begin to guide them out of the pain these evils bring.

Permission to Go

When pharaoh awoke and realized that he had lost his firstborn child and that every firstborn had died in every Egyptian home in his kingdom, he broke down. He had been beaten. He had been beaten so badly that his resources had been totally depleted: no pride, no wit, no might, no majesty, no more playing God, no more tricks, no more orders, burdens, or deaths. He was now a broken man ruling over a battered and broken land. With a wrenching pain in his heart and emptiness in his stomach, choking back his tears, pharaoh told Moses and Israel to go. "Go! Take everybody, take your women and children, take your possessions, take whatever you need and leave us." The Egyptians encouraged the Israelites to leave quickly by giving them whatever they wanted and helping them along, because the Egyptians were afraid they would all soon die if another plague were to come.

Spiritually, after we have endured plague after plague, whether that is within our imaginations or in our actual lives, something finally happens to cause the pharaoh inside of us to drop to his knees and cry, "Enough is enough! I can't take it anymore. How many people must I hurt? How much suffering must I endure? I've got to change. Anything, anything is better than this. There must be another way!"

At that point, when the pharaoh inside submits, move forward. Immediately! Follow the new voice of Moses and Aaron within and start out that night toward a new life. Otherwise, pharaoh may change his mind, yet again. When you finally recognize, for example, that you must change your habits, begin that very moment to start a life without them. Don't say, "I'll begin tomorrow." Do it immediately. When you realize you need to change a relationship or seek help for your problems or simply begin again, don't wait a

few weeks to start. Your pharaoh will rebound into the same trap
he has always led you into. When you realize that you've been leading a superficial life without God, love, or spirituality, take the steps
that very moment to begin a new way and a new search for what is
missing. If you delay, you will not change. Your foolish ego—your
inner pharaoh—won't hit bottom and remain humbled forever. It
will gather its forces to take charge once again, pursuing you, only
to thrust you, once again, under its dominion.

The Israelites moved out immediately, taking with them anything of value they could get from the Egyptians, taking their gold,
silver, and jewelry. We too, when we leave our materialistic way of
life behind, can take what is valuable. Egypt, as a representation of
secular learning and science, isn't all bad. It's the slavery, the
bondage, the pain of a worldly outlook alone that we must escape
from. But when we embark on a search for spirituality, we don't
have to abandon our valuable scientific and secular knowledge. We
can take what is good about Egypt with us.

It is a mistake to think that when one decides to pursue spirituality, he or she must sacrifice intellectual pursuits or common sense.
The spiritual life and outlook do not forbid science or common
sense. We can take from the Egyptians as we make our escape. We
can continue to make use of what science and technology tell us,
tempered with the resolution that we are not going to rely on them
alone. We have a new guide now, Moses, and the God of Moses.
We foster a gentle perception of the divine reality and guidance.
We hear the voice of truth in what the Divine tells us through
Moses. We use the Egyptians, but we also seek first the kingdom of
God (and his righteousness for a change), and only then are all
these things added to us.

The night of their escape, the children of Israel were led by God
in an unusual form. He did not appear in the form of a man to lead
them, nor did he speak to them in a clear voice. Rather, he led them
with a pillar of fire by night and a pillar of cloud by day. The Divine
leads us the same way. When we first move forward to a new life of

spiritual growth, we still do not have a clear concept of whom God is, or what life is all about, or even where we are going. Our image of God is a cloudy image, even in the brightest moments of the day. In the nighttime of our lives, when our perception of spiritual life is dark, we can't see the divine plan or guidance at all. We only sense the divine love, that burning fire, which leads us onward toward freedom.

As we follow this pillar, we might say to ourselves, "I don't know where I am going in my life, but I know I must get out of here!" We can't envision what lies ahead. We know little about the promised land and its delights, but we do sense that there must be a better way of life than we've experienced so far, held captive in the state of spiritual bondage. Sometimes, in the beginning of our spiritual growth, we have no perception of our path or our destination, except for a slight sense that we are loved by something higher than ourselves. We might find ourselves, in our darkest hour of temptation, for example, repeating, "I know God loves me, and I need that love." Fortified with a knowledge like that, we move away from pharaoh and Egypt toward that feeling of love. That's following the fire.

Keep Moving Forward

As the children of Israel fled Egypt toward freedom, pharaoh— true to form—changed his mind. He said, "What have we done? We have let the Israelites go and have lost their services" (Exodus 14:5). He gathered up his armies and six hundred chariots and went off to stop these people. Soon the children of Israel began to hear the roar of the Egyptians' chariots in hot pursuit. They began to panic in fear. As they tried to escape, they came to a huge and impenetrable sea! They were trapped! The Red Sea stood before them and pharaoh's army approached from behind. They cried out to Moses and prepared to die.

What does this represent within us? Our first spiritual steps carry us forward a little, but then our ego begins to change its mind.

As we move toward a new way of life, suddenly, like the Israelites, we come before a huge and impenetrable sea. We feel trapped. The water, here, symbolizes an overwhelming burden of the truth—that on our own, we cannot move forward. On our own, we cannot change.

It's a common experience. We take our first steps to improve, to escape an old habit or thought pattern, and confront this barrier almost instantly. A voice inside starts telling us that our effort is futile. We wonder how we can change. We thought we knew the way, but have known only the slavery of our own ego, only the rule of our selfish impulses, our fears, the taskmasters back home. A voice inside says we can't change!

Once, as I prepared a talk about the parting of the Red Sea, a young man wandered into my office to chat. I explained to him the Israelites' plight, and he suddenly jumped up, gleefully recognizing the story's inherent truth. He exclaimed, "That's me! I am right there at the brink of that sea. I've been trying to change my life and something keeps telling me that it's hopeless, that it's impossible! What do I do next?"

Unfortunately, it's easier said than done. It takes a lot of courage. To trust in a power greater than ourselves—a power we have not known, seen, or possibly not yet experienced—may be the most difficult move we've ever made. But we must listen to Moses, the Word within us, the one part of us that seems to speak the truth. Even as we hear the roar of pharaoh's chariot wheels, even as we are taunted by the lapping waves of the Red Sea, we must listen and obey the voice of truth within.

Moses, the truth within, speaks to us strongly. He tells us to stop murmuring and listen to him. "Do not be afraid. Stand still, and see the salvation of the Lord, which he will accomplish for you today. . . . The Lord will fight for you, and you shall hold your peace" (Exodus 14:13-14). We realize that we can't change. Left to our own devices, we are stuck in bondage forever. But a power greater than ourselves *can* deliver us from this predicament. God, as we understand him, will make a miracle happen. If we move forward, if we listen to the truth and uphold what little good we do know in life, the power of the Divine will split this barrier in two and we will be free!

Moses tells the people to move forward. Move forward into the sea? Into the darkness? Into the abyss? Yes, because it won't stay that way for long! And then Moses raises that special rod, which represents the power of what we know to be good in our lives, and the miracle begins to happen. Instead of casting it down, as Aaron did as a warning of what could be, Moses lifts that rod up. He elevates it above all else. It's as if God were saying, "Don't just stand there. Move forward. Take the good you do know and raise it up on high. Lift it up above yourself and your own concerns. Make it a priority in your life." And if we do that, if we take action and make goodness a priority, an east wind will come out of the sky and split that sea. Power from above will break the barrier in two. Suddenly there will be a vision, a way, an answer to prayers of desperation. We will see the other side, a way out of our predicament to new freedom. We can cross over. All is not hopeless. It's a miracle!

Imagine the Israelites' descent into that valley of dry land that was the Red Sea. The walls of the sea stand tall on either side of them, the invisible dams to break at any moment. Only a profound trust in their God could compel them to walk straight into the sea. And we too must trust. We must move forward. After all, we can see the opposite banks of the sea. We must trust that we will emerge unharmed into a new way of life, a life we recently doubted could exist.

After the Israelites cross the sea, they stop to look back toward Egypt. They see pharaoh's armies, his horsemen and chariots, driving forward in a rage and fury, descending into the basin to pursue Israel. Moses raises his hands toward the sea and suddenly the swelling waters return with a crash. Men and horses scream, chariot wheels and bones shatter, and the Israelites hear the last gasps and gurgles of hundreds of souls as tons of water bury them. And then, almost in an instant, silence falls over all. The Egyptians are dead. The madness is over. Israel stands stunned, shocked at the sight of utter and instantaneous destruction.

Pharaoh's armies are destroyed. The Bible never states that pharaoh went down with his troops. He may have. We don't know. On a deeper level it would make sense that he did not drown with his army. We never completely get rid of our ego. The ego is part of our character. But it can lose its power over us. This picture of the Egyptian army coming to destruction is a vision we have of what life would have been like under our ego's rule. Even as Israel turned to face Egypt, we too turn, look back in reflection at what might have been. We see the truth about our ego, that left to itself it will destroy us. We imagine the hell, the destruction, the damnation. We say to ourselves, "How could I have ever been like that? Look where I was headed! Look what could have happened to me!"

For example, the young addict may finally have moved across that sea out of chemical dependence and abuse. He finally breaks through the illusion that he cannot live without it. No longer identifying with his personal pharaoh or Egypt, he looks back to see the Egyptians that drove him to this abuse day in and day out plunge themselves furiously into the abyss, crushed by the waters, destroyed. He imagines himself down there, buried under tons of water. That could have been he. If he had continued this abuse, he would have destroyed himself. And perhaps his family, or his friends, would have been floating down there with him too, victims of his madness. But God saved him from that scenario. He no longer identifies with pharaoh. He now follows Moses, and the God of Moses.

Or, again, think of the woman who suffers from a codependent relationship in this circumstance. Perhaps she finally gets up the courage to move forward, to join a support group, to lay down certain new laws of decency and human behavior to her husband. She makes a commitment not to enable, or save, or control anymore. She demands that he get help. At first, she was quite anxious; that first day of her new life was a scary one. There were some troubled spots, but with trust in a new power greater than herself, she managed not to play her husband's game. She let go and stood up for herself and crossed that border.

Later, perhaps a couple of days or weeks after her decision, she stops to reflect on her life and the hell she had put up with for so long. No, she's not in the clear yet. Her husband is talking about treatment, but is not there yet. But she clearly recognizes that she has begun to change. When she looks back at that hell she lived in not so long ago, she is shocked by what she sees. She recognizes that if she had not taken steps to change, to stop controlling, rescuing, and engaging in other destructive behavior, she thinks she would have collapsed, or even committed suicide, plunging into the turbulent water. She breathes a sigh of relief as she witnesses the Egyptians disappear under the deluge. She no longer identifies with her old way of life or thinking. She has crossed a spiritual barrier and is ready to move on.

We can witness as well the Egyptians' destruction in our struggle to rid ourselves of our own character defects. We may have broken the bonds of our own rage, the anger we have unsuccessfully been trying to curb for years. But after we have learned to trust a power greater than self and to move forward, we witness a change. As the tendency toward anger breaks, we look back at our past habit, and we imagine the destruction it could have wrought. Our anger could have spiraled us into further destruction, hurting loved ones, really wounding them. But the waters are silent now. We've crossed to the other side. Pharaoh is powerless. His armies are dead, and a new day dawns.

We, like the Israelites, embrace a belief in our new God. We have experienced his power: we were trapped and he delivered us. We stand in awe of the destruction that was, the destruction that could have been. We are free for the first time from the bondage of our egos. We have escaped the fantasy and illusion of our pride and intellect. We are free, indeed! We look once more at Egypt, beyond the still waters of the Red Sea. We turn our eyes to Moses with wonder and respect. We don't know exactly where we are going now, but we've been told it's going to be good. We look toward the vast wilderness ahead, toward the distant horizon. Beyond that horizon, a hope and a dream summon us, entreat us, to begin the journey toward a land we can call our own.

Exercises

1. What action, habit, or pattern of thought has hurt you in the past or hurts you now? Analyze why you hold onto it. Imagine the worst negative consequences that would have to happen before you'd consent to let go and change.

2. When you experience weakness and doubt, think of a simple good deed you could easily do for someone, and then go and do it. How does your internal state change? What other good actions can you immediately add to your life?

3. Do you experience God? Spend one day really looking for God in your life. Don't change your routine, just keep an eye out. Can you see God in nature, in others' faces, in your memories? Can you hear God in music, in the voices of friends, family, even strangers? Can you feel God in the weather, in another's touch, in your life's direction? How does your perception of God change after you have spent a day looking for him? Will you look for him again tomorrow?

So Moses brought Israel from the Red Sea; then they went out into the Wilderness of Shur. And they went three days in the wilderness and found no water. Now when they came to Marah, they could not drink the waters of Marah, for they were bitter. . . . And the people murmured against Moses, saying, "What shall we drink?" So he cried out to the Lord, and the Lord showed him a piece of wood; and when he cast it into the waters, the waters were made sweet. There he made a statute and an ordinance for them. And there he tested them and said, "If you diligently heed the voice of the Lord your God and do what is right in his sight and give ear to his commandments and keep all his statutes, I will put none of the diseases on you which I have brought on the Egyptians. For I am the Lord who heals you." Then they came to Elim, where there were twelve wells of water and seventy palm trees; so they camped there by the waters.   Exodus 15:22-27

CHAPTER THREE

Bitter Realizations

Bitter Waters

Waters mean truths and the perception of them.

Apocalypse Explained 283:13

Wilderness Way

Moses led the children of Israel away from the Red Sea, into the wilderness, toward the promised land. The journey would be a long one (longer than anyone, including Moses, would have imagined!). But the Israelites' ecstasy over their new freedom from captivity drove them forward. The words of a song, found in Exodus 15:1–18, that Moses and the children of Israel sang to the Lord reflect their delight:

I will sing to the Lord,
For he has triumphed gloriously .
The Lord is my strength and song,
And he has become my salvation;
He is my God, and I will praise him.
Pharaoh's chariots and his army
He has cast into the sea.
You stretched out your right hand;
The earth swallowed them.
You in your mercy have led forth
The people whom you have redeemed:
You have guided them in your strength

45

To your holy habitation.
The Lord shall reign forever and ever.

We too, after the Divine delivers us from the personal bondage of egotism, sing inward praises to our newfound God and enjoy the ecstasy of our newfound freedom. We too laugh at the pharaoh we have escaped and praise the power greater than ourselves who has pulled us out of the pit of bondage. We are eager to learn more about this power. We are eager to live in that "holy habitation" that God has promised. Like the Israelites, we can sense that soon we will inhabit a wonderful land and settle there, fulfilled, happy, and peaceful.

Wouldn't it be nice if life were really like that? If only a person could make one great move toward a spiritual life and achieve that life instantaneously! But Moses led the children of Israel into the wilderness for three days without tasting, let alone seeing, a drop of water. Imagine three days of dry dust, rocks, occasional shrubs here and there, uncomfortable sun, whipping wind, and all that sand. Paradise? This was beginning to resemble hell. The people murmured, "Where is the water?" A fair enough question! They had trusted in God to save them from their state of bondage and lead them toward a better life, and they spend the first three days thirsty and searching the desert for signs of water.

But isn't that the reality of life? When people first begin to escape the bonds of ego and their own destructive tendencies, they don't immediately enter a new and spiritual existence. At first, like Israel, they do celebrate their new freedom and vast potential for growth. But soon they realize that they are not in heaven. They are wandering in a wilderness. They realize that they don't have any water. They thirst. They need spiritual water for this journey.

Water, as we have seen, symbolizes a type of truth, the living truth that will sustain us. This cool, refreshing, life-giving spiritual substance is sparse in that first track of wilderness. We probably assumed we had packed enough water for the journey toward spiritual life, but the water from Egypt seems to dry up and disappear immediately. What we thought we knew about life is not enough to sustain us now. It hardly counts for anything. We might have expected to find some kind of sustenance out here in the wilderness, not too many miles from Egypt, but we find nothing, certainly not what we would call truth. Answers to our problems are not scattered like wells in the ground here and there ready to be tapped at will and applied to our lives.

When we first begin this spiritual journey toward a new way of life, we don't have all the answers. In fact, we have very few, if any, answers that we find truly satisfying. We have entered a new territory. We don't know what is right and wrong, and we have no map. We can't gauge what goals or ideas are important, which will give us hope and sustenance, which will truly refresh and satisfy our lives. We simply don't have enough truth to sustain us.

This absence of truth is illustrated in daily life. A new worker, for instance, will feel lost in a wilderness, longing to understand the essential components of the job, thirsting for knowledge about how to execute the job correctly. When a colleague of mine became principal of a high school, he said that for weeks he felt that he was wandering in a wilderness, not just wondering how to be a good principal, but actually panicking for knowledge about how to run the school. Even opening the mail presented a challenge. His slight understanding of the job wasn't enough to help him decide what mail should be saved or what discarded, what mail should be acted on immediately, or what mail forwarded to others. As he gained experience in the job, this dilemma sorted itself out. But in the beginning, he experienced that thirst in the wilderness in his new job.

This thirst can also be experienced in marriage. A newly married couple enjoys the first honeymoon days of marriage. Like Moses and the children of Israel singing and dancing with joy, the couple revels in their new state, celebrating the new journey they are beginning together. Many couples soon discover, however, that they have no clue about how to make this marriage work. They don't have the answers or even the instincts to work their way out of quarrels, negotiate domestic responsibilities, raise children, or deal with hundreds of other marital puzzles. Especially when new problems arise, they can feel that they are in a wilderness; their utter lack of knowledge is like a thirst, unsatisfied while they struggle for answers.

When my wife Cathy and I had our first child, we were thrust quickly into a very deep thirst for answers. I'm sure most first-time parents feel that way. How do you raise children? How come we never learned that in graduate school? The birth of this new and fragile being was terrifying enough. But when the doctors dropped him in our laps with a bottle, a bag of diapers, and some Wipy Dipes, I knew a new kind of terror for the first time. Maybe someone at the hospital had forgotten to give us the instruction booklet! Nevertheless, we learned together and did our best. Most of us do survive the ordeal and learn, but the beginning of parenthood can feel like a dry and thirsty new state.

The thirst represented in this biblical story is felt most vividly in people's spiritual lives. They move forward, escape old ways, enter a new way of life, but find that they don't have the answers they need. They journey not to paradise, but into a void, a dry and dusty wasteland. They can feel lost spiritually and begin to thirst for some answers.

Some might labor to escape the fears they have suffered from, but with little success. They may engage in a conversation with themselves similar to this:

"How do I stop the fear from coming back?"

"I don't know."

"What do I do when I come into new situations that will bring the fear on?"

"I don't know."

"How do I stop it if I begin to feel it rise up within me?"

"Beats me."

"Where does this fear come from? Is part of it good? Should I be afraid sometimes but not at other times?"

"Well, these are all good questions, but I don't have a clue!"

"Is there anybody else in here I can talk to? God, help me! Where is the truth?"

A person might be working hard to escape manipulating or controlling others. Frank, for example, has progressed steadily toward not dominating others, but soon is stopped because he lacks the knowledge to continue his progress. He has always been a controller at work, and has spent many years forcing other people who must work under his control. He has never given his subordinates enough independence in doing their work. But now he is trying. He has stopped monitoring them every five minutes and demanding changes, but he doesn't know how to react if they really need assistance. After all, they may not have liked his control but they became used to it. Many questions puzzle Frank. At what point should he get involved in their work? What is the difference between being a supervisor and being a manipulator? How can one supervise and not manipulate? And what does Frank do with all the free time now that he isn't policing others? He used to be decisive, but now he doesn't know what direction to take. He thirsts for the truth.

Our general condition of spirituality can leave us feeling similarly lost. We may have thought that we had most of the answers before, when we lived the old way. Now, after we've decided to change our life, we realize we know nothing beyond that. We are certain that we want to change. But we don't know anything at all about God, or about ourselves, or about goodness or love or friendship or happiness or anything about anything at all. We begin to search for the truth about life and for quite a while we come up high and dry. We just don't have the answers.

Bitter Waters

God does not abandon us to die of thirst in the wilderness. He leads us, as he led the Israelites, to tranquil waters and he restores our souls. But relief does not come without some painful recognition on our part, not without the bitter waters of Marah.

The Bible states that, after a three-day search for water, Moses and Israel finally happened along some pools of water called "the waters of Marah." The Hebrew word *Marah* means "bitter." Imagine the people's wild and excited eyes when they discover this water. They must have dropped everything and run forward. Perhaps they dove into the pools, submerged their heads to suck in the refreshing sustenance: perhaps they knelt beside the water, cupping it into their hands, raising it to their lips and open mouths in trembling excitement—but only for a moment. Immediately, bursts of water spewed from their mouths, their faces became twisted and colorless in pain; perhaps even some began to convulse and regurgitate. These waters were undrinkable! They were too bitter to be swallowed.

These waters of Marah, the first waters the Israelites encountered, represent the first life-giving truths you and I encounter on our new journey toward spirituality. These first truths are not pleasant. They are bitter recognitions about self, about the negative effect we have had on others, about how we don't really understand God, about making uncomfortable changes in order to achieve spirituality. We come upon these truths as if by accident. We immediately long to absorb their healing power, to drink them up and ponder them in our conscious minds and to let their refreshing qualities sustain our drive for progress. But they are all so bitter, so hard to swallow.

One of the bitterest truths tells us that we are merely mortal human beings. We are not gods. Back in our state of bondage, our egos thought our intelligence was supreme, godlike in its abilities to understand life and to control it. But now we know that pharaoh is not God but a fool. We have come to the waters of realization that we must change on a deeper level than we'd thought. Familiar thought patterns must be changed; comfortable habits must be broken. These thoughts and habits have brought us some delight, even though they may have been destructive. We may realize that some apologies must be given. Burned-down bridges must be rebuilt. It won't be easy; in fact, it will be painful. But it is the next step as we improve our lives.

Some religious truths can appear bitter and difficult to accept. For instance, the truth about forgiveness can seem a bitter teaching. Most religions tell us to forgive our debtors and to wish well to our enemies. This can be hard to take. Even though we may recognize that anger and resentment only hurt us, true forgiveness may, at times, be too bitter a pill to swallow and incorporate into our lives. And traditional teachings about sexual morality can also leave a bitter taste in one's mouth. For example, a young man may spend several years living a wild and promiscuous sexual life and feeling like a slave to his desires. After his initial escape, though, he may long for a new path, to find love rather than lust, to commit to a relationship rather than to commit fornication or adultery. But abstinence before marriage, or commitment to one person, or sharing rather than using can seem impossible to him. He realizes that these teachings are truths that lead to a better and more orderly life, but they are so hard to take. How can he change to a life of love, order, and responsibility after years of lust, disorder, and neglect?

Sometimes a sudden revelation about self can serve as bitter waters. I know this has been true for me. One especially difficult drink of bitter waters came to my lips as I pushed two of my friends to do something my way one day, and it backfired. In my youth I had been a guitar player in several rock bands. But when I married and became a minister, I sold my guitar and amplifier for some food and clothing. When I took my first job as a youth pastor, the local teens found out I played the guitar and procured an inexpensive guitar and an old amplifier for my enjoyment. Two friends of mine, one a professional musician and another who had just begun to learn to play drums, were interested in playing together for fun once a week, just to live out some latent rock'n'roll fantasies to, I suppose, heal the rock star within.

After several weeks of playing together, I heard that the local high school was having a party and that it was planning on using a DJ and

recorded music to accompany the dancing. Immediately I thought
of the idea of playing a few songs for the teens. I thought this was a
fabulous idea because my experience told me that every teen loves
the sound of a live guitar and drums, and we would certainly be a hit.

To my surprise, my two musician friends didn't see it that way.
They felt we just hadn't practiced enough, and we'd flop. Of
course, I wouldn't take "no" for an answer—I didn't just *think*
we'd be a big hit; I *knew* we would be a big hit! With such strong
conviction, I launched into what can only be called Gestapo tactics.
I actually separated my friends into two rooms and began to work
them over one by one, convincing first one and then the other, that
we could not lose, that the "kids were going to go nuts!" After about
forty-five minutes, I broke them down. They finally saw the folly
of their thinking and the clear reason of mine. That night we set up
for the high school party in the gym. The room was full of teens,
some came up and marvelled over our guitars and amps. I was excited, and my friends even began to apologize for their reservations,
seeing these teens take special notice of their musical instruments
and equipment. We were given a wonderful introduction by the DJ
and began to play.

As the guitars whaled and the amplifiers roared to the beat of the
drums, the kids jumped up and down on the dance floor and
screamed in excitement. I knew they would. I smiled over at my
friend, the drummer, and laid down a few more riffs on the guitar.
But what soon followed became what I could only describe as the
performer's nightmare. One by one the students raised their hands
to cover their ears and headed for the doors. In a matter of three
minutes they emptied the room, leaving behind two students who
happened to be babysitters for my children, and who obviously felt
sorry for me and wanted to show their support.

We bombed, just as my friends said we would. I cannot describe
to you the humiliation I felt in that situation and how sorry I was
that I had manipulated my friends into playing. But what struck me
more than anything was how right I thought I was and how wrong

I turned out to be. I was so sorry, and somehow my friends were kind enough to forgive me. But I learned something that evening. I drank the bitter waters that revealed to me so clearly that I could feel certain about something and be completely wrong. I saw how I could manipulate and recognized how wrong I was to do so. The truth was hard to swallow, but necessary for my spiritual growth. From then on I began to make it a priority in my life to give people freedom to disagree and always to recognize that, no matter how confident I may feel, I may be completely wrong. This lesson ended up helping me a great deal in my spiritual growth.

Often, in times of spiritual temptation, challenge, and growth, the bitter truths are the ones we need to hear the most. They taste bitter because they do make our life uncomfortable. They challenge us to think differently from what we had previously. They challenge us to change what we might not want to change. They illuminate the reality of our lives, washing away the illusions to reveal the bitter truth of our existence. We need these truths badly, and we need to learn how to accept them and use them.

Waters Made Sweet

In the story from Exodus, Moses and Israel did not leave behind those bitter waters; rather, Moses cried out to his God for help with this predicament. And God answered him with a strange set of instructions. He told Moses to pick up a piece of wood, or what some translations call a tree, and throw it into the water, and the water will become sweet. That must have seemed like an outlandish request. Why a piece of wood? Why throw it in the water? But when you're that thirsty, does it really matter what the command is? Why not try it and see what happens? And so they did.

Perhaps the spiritual symbolism here will seem as outlandish as God's request, but if you are thirsty enough, try it and see what happens. Moses was instructed to take a piece of wood and throw it in the water. We know that water symbolizes truth. What does the wood represent? Goodness, a very natural or earthly goodness.

Remember that the wooden rod that Moses and Aaron used represented the power of good in one's life. This piece of wood has a similar significance. Wood comes from trees. In fact, some translations of the Bible call that piece of wood a "tree." A tree symbolizes a perception of goodness. A tree absorbs the sun's rays and renders them useful. Isn't that what human perception does? It receives the divine light, God's wisdom that shines down on us, and produces good from it. A strong and healthy tree represents a strong and healthy perception of God's goodness, presence, and sunshine. Even a branch from a tree, being just part of the whole, would be a slight perception of goodness, just seeing part of the picture. This particular piece of wood or tree symbolizes a very dim sense of goodness, and our slightest action to bring that goodness into our lives.

Keeping this in mind, we remember Moses' wandering the mountains of Midian. How did God speak to him there? He spoke to Moses through a burning bush, which, like trees, also symbolized a perception of God's presence and love. It represented the perception one can have that God exists and that he cares for us and will deliver us from bondage. The piece of wood, or tree, that Moses was instructed to throw into the water symbolizes both a perception of goodness and an action toward goodness. This particular wooden object isn't burning or doing anything unusual. No immediate presence of God can be found in it, no burning fire of love. It looks like a simple, useless piece of wood. But it has power if we use it.

So what do we do with this wood? Simple: throw it into the water. Take that sense of good that you do have in your life and add it to that bitter truth. Take action to live by that truth and it will become sweet. Ask yourself, "What is good about this particular truth that seems so bitter? What is good about forgiveness? What is good about morality? Where will they lead me? Can I recognize their benefits?" Look for the good in the bitter truth, and once you find it, follow it. Live the truth, splash right in, and the truth will become drinkable and sustain you.

Remember this principle: if the water is bitter, throw some wood into it. If a truth is hard to swallow, mix in a little good. Find the good that grows out of that truth. Ask yourself what goodness that truth leads to. Meditate on it, and then put the two together, live the truth in question and it will become sweet.

What does this mean in our daily life? Take, for example, the concept of forgiveness. At first, the truth that forgiveness is something commanded by God may be a bitter mouthful to swallow. The last thing we may want to do is forgive someone who has hurt us. But we should look for the good that grows out of that teaching: that forgiveness leads to healing, to reconciliation, and to a state of peace. We should throw the wood into the water by putting those two ideas together, first in our minds, and then in our life. We should splash right in with a desire for healing and reconciliation, and then begin to forgive.

When we live by the truth, it then becomes sweet. When we learn to forgive, suddenly it doesn't seem like such a distasteful teaching anymore. We see that forgiveness isn't something to shun or spurn. In fact, forgiving others soothes our inner burning and discontent. It brings a new feeling of peace and a sense of inner tranquility and contentment. The bitter waters, after throwing a little good into them, have become sweet and refreshing.

For the young man who is trying to bring his love life into order, the truths about sexual morality, responsibility, and love may seem difficult, if not impossible, to accept. But when he finds the good that can grow out of these truths—that, for instance, he can learn to build a lasting relationship based on new principles of love and friendship—then he builds inner support for his new way of life. Then, when he begins to change his life by concentrating on the good in these teachings, the whole philosophy soon sweetens.

After he has lived by new moral truths, he may realize that these teachings don't hinder him but set him free. He finds himself free from an unquenchable hunger for the flesh he never realized had plagued him so thoroughly. Suddenly this type of hunger disappears. He doesn't feel so driven by animal instinct anymore, nor feel the guilt of acting on it. In fact, since he has resolved to seek a meaningful, caring, loving relationship, all of his relationships have noticeably improved. The people in his new life care, respect him and themselves, and are willing to love, even as he is now willing to love.

For me, and my experience with the rock band that bombed, I took those bitter realizations about myself—that I could be very wrong when I felt very right, and that I could be a terrible manipulator—and tried to use those truths for good. I threw some wood into the bitter waters by promising myself that I would take time to listen to others, that I would respect other people's freedom. Since then I have grown much in this area over the years, and this hard lesson has helped my life and relationships get better, not worse, become sweeter rather than more bitter.

When you and I, like Israel, come to bitter waters in our lives, it may seem strange to find the nearest piece of wood and throw it into the water. But that is what God has commanded, and he knows that it will bring us healing. In fact, after Israel drinks of the water now sweetened by the wood, God says, "If you diligently heed the voice of the Lord your God and do what is right in his sight, . . . I will put none of the diseases on you which I brought on the Egyptians. For I am the Lord who heals you" (Exodus 15:26).

It is interesting to note that God refers to the Egyptian plagues and assures Israel that these plagues will not recur if Israel obeys, because God will be their healer. One wonders why God would mention plagues and healings, since in the story the Israelites had suffered no plague and hadn't been sick. God's words make more sense, though, when read allegorically. For God speaks not only to Israel, but to us as individuals, not only to the Israelite within us (the good part of us that is willing to follow God), but to the Egyptian who suffered (the more earthly part that would not obey). He talks not only to our obedient spiritual selves but to the external part of us that endured the plagues, to the part within us that is not only thirsty, but sick and lame and badly needs his help. He addresses our whole character.

God's message is a new one for us. He tells us in our inmost thoughts that if we obey his rules and follow his guidance, we will be healed and we will be happy. Before we tasted the bitter truths of Marah, we didn't see any real cause and effect in our lives. We grasped each challenge separately: we knew we had to flee Egypt; we knew that life must consist of more than bondage to a worldly existence; we discovered God in a hope and a dream that promised a better way; we pursued that promise on faith alone. Only now, after tasting some life-giving truth, do we begin to understand God. We have learned that the Divine not only exists, but that God is a healer, that God wants only for us to be happy, and that we will find healing and happiness by following his ways. This is a new perception to us. We are beginning to understand, if only for a fleeting moment, what life is about.

An Oasis in the Wilderness

How uncanny that, after all the fuss the author of the book of Exodus spent on the bitter waters, he abruptly and without transition, writes, "Then they came to Elim, where there were twelve wells of water and seventy palm trees; so they camped there by the waters" (Exodus 15:27). It almost sounds as if the children of Israel could have simply looked beyond the waters of Marah a couple of hundred yards to have seen an oasis, with all the pure and refreshing water one ever desired, and plenty of shady palms as well.

This immediate discovery of Elim may seem puzzling on a literal level, but it fits neatly into our spiritual paradigm. After we accept this initially bitter truth into our lives, we are rewarded by a period of consolation. We find rest. Our spiritual understanding seems to have grown and matured overnight. Great wells of water appear before us, new truths, new clear perspectives on different aspects of our lives. We draw water, at will, gleaning truth from our newly discovered inner resources. And the palms that surround the oasis aren't branches or shrubs, or dead pieces of wood lying here and there, but majestic palms that stretch toward the sun. Our perception of life has grown so much and so quickly.

Perhaps you have felt such a state. You've worked hard to overcome some spiritual obstacle within your life. You've struggled to learn a new way of thought, accept new truth, and to live a new life. At first it is quite a struggle; but when you overcome, you find yourself in a time of great consolation. Things just seem to start going right for you. You can't really point to any outward circumstance that would bring you such a feeling of well-being; but, nevertheless, you *do* feel it. You are content, feel rested, and have a wonderful sense of peace and tranquility. You are able to enjoy life like never before, and it all seems to be a gift. Even though you know this sense of well-being won't last forever, that more work needs to be done in your spiritual life, for now it sure is fun. You stick up a hammock between two palms, sip a cool cup of water, close your eyes, and enjoy the light breeze blowing through the shaded trees.

Life is good in this wilderness paradise, at least for the time being. But we haven't yet reached the promised land. We continue to exist out in the middle of nowhere, spiritually; we camp by the oasis, rest in this temporary state of tranquility and consolation, until we are ready to move on toward new challenges. We know that soon we must leave this paradise to find that new way of life promised to us in our dreams. But for now we rest, comforted in Elim.

Exercises

1. Become an expert. If you have a problem (addiction, codependency, fear, marriage trouble, etc.), read a book about it. The book may not radically change your life, but it will begin to give you a much-needed perspective.

2. *What bitter truths in your life are hard to swallow? How will accepting them work to heal you? Begin a new action or thought process that will help you accept truth and start the healing.*

3. *Do you need a rest from your spiritual search? Take some time out for yourself to relax and enjoy a break in your wilderness paradise. Can you give yourself a break?*

READINGS

And they journeyed from Elim, and all the congregation of the children of Israel came to the Wilderness of Sin, which is between Elim and Sinai, on the fifteenth day of the second month after they departed from the land of Egypt. Then the whole congregation of the children of Israel murmured against Moses and Aaron in the wilderness. And the children of Israel said to them, "Oh, that we had died by the hand of the Lord in the land of Egypt, when we sat by the flesh pots and when we ate bread to the full! For you have brought us out into this wilderness to kill this whole assembly with hunger." Exodus 16:1-3

And the Lord spoke to Moses saying, "I have heard the murmurings of the children of Israel. Speak to them, saying, 'At twilight you shall eat meat, and in the morning you shall be filled with bread. And you shall know that I am the Lord your God.'" So it was that quails came up at evening and covered the camp, and in the morning dew lay all around the camp. And when the layer of dew lifted, there, on the surface of the wilderness, was a small round substance, as fine as frost on the ground. So when the children of Israel saw it, they said to one another, "What is it?" For they did not know what it was. And Moses said to them, "This is the bread which the Lord has given you to eat."   Exodus 16:9-15

And the house of Israel called its name Manna. And it was like white coriander seed, and the taste of it was like wafers made with honey. . . . And the children of Israel ate manna for forty years, until they came to an inhabited land; they ate manna until they came to the border of the land of Canaan. Exodus 16:31, 35

CHAPTER FOUR

Spiritual Sustenance

Bread from Heaven

'This is the bread which the Lord has given you to eat' means that this is the good which will be taken in and will make up a new life; in the supreme sense, that this is the Lord in you.

Arcana Coelestia 8464

The Struggle of Life

The children of Israel left the oasis at Elim to begin a journey through the wilderness that would last forty years. For forty years they wandered across the dry plains, between the mountains, and through the barren valleys, looking for paradise. For four decades they hungered and thirsted in the wilderness. During this time of trial, hardship, and temptation, they truly grew as a people, not just in number, but in every way. They learned to have faith in God, that he would feed and lead them. They learned to rely, not on themselves alone, but on a power greater than self who would never betray them. In the wilderness they grew from slaves into freedom fighters. They learned dignity, as they grew into a great people, a nation. But this extensive growth took forty years of wandering and temptation. In fact, without this period of struggle in the wilderness, they would not have grown so fully.

The same is true in personal spiritual growth. People spend much of their lives, not in a state of paradisal bliss, but in a wilderness looking for bliss. So much of life is a search, and sometimes a struggle. It would be nice to tell you that, while you are in your personal wilderness, you could snap your heels together, like Dorothy in *The Wizard of Oz*, and suddenly awaken in paradise, happy and alive, mumbling in euphoric delirium, "There's no place like home. There's no place like home." You may have heard that you can find instant paradise by repeating certain phrases, or learning special psychological techniques, or sleeping with certain rocks under your pillow, or drinking a certain formula found in a hidden vault in the cave of an ancient reclusive guru. People have been selling the quick-fix spiritual life for years. But, sad to say, the quick fix is a lie. Those who sell it are spiritual swindlers. There is no quick fix to life. Life is mostly a search in the wilderness; and through that search, growth takes place.

Now, that is not to say that the goal of paradise isn't real. The promised land is real. Spiritual growth can be attained. Happiness, peace of mind, and tranquility can be achieved. But these aren't instantaneously granted by the Divine. The children of Israel couldn't take the next plane out of Egypt to Jerusalem. They had to make the journey, and that journey permitted them to grow, and they grew through pain and struggle. But the result of that struggle was paradise. Crossing that wilderness brought them to the promised land. In the end, the promised land that flowed with milk and honey became their home. The goal is real, but so is the work to achieve that goal.

While we wander in the wilderness of life, the Divine does care for us. As the stories have illustrated, and as we will see in the story of the manna, God, as we understand him, nourishes us in times of thirst and hunger. He gives us the sustenance we need. Like the children of Israel, when we thirst, we come upon water; when we hunger, we are freely given food by our God. He does not leave us spiritually hungry or thirsty, but the hunger and thirst are part of the journey and part of the process of spiritual growth.

Longing for the Fleshpots

As the children of Israel wandered, their supplies from Egypt dwindled. Not only did they run out of water, but they ran out of food. As their empty stomachs began to shrink and ache for even the tiniest morsel of sustenance, they started to dream of the food they once ate in Egypt. They began to murmur against Moses saying, "Oh, that we had died by the hand of the Lord in the land of Egypt, when we sat by the fleshpots and when we ate bread to the full! For you have brought us out into this wilderness to kill this whole assembly with hunger" (Exodus 16:3).

Does the Israelites' dissension sound familiar? You move forward toward a new life, abandoning some of your old destructive ways. But eventually you begin to feel that you are missing something. You become hungry for that good old pleasure you used to enjoy living the old way, when your bad habits and destructive ways of living would give you so much pleasure. You don't recall the pain of slavery associated with them. Out in the wilderness you may, at times, feel no pleasure or delight. You left your old ways on the promise that happiness would come to you—"a great reward" you were told. But the reward is nowhere in sight. You can feel empty inside. You can feel no joy or delight.

The food that Israel longs for symbolizes the spiritual food that we must eat regularly to survive. It represents delight, a sense of pleasure, well-being. We need to feel good, to feel happiness and some delight in our lives in order to continue to function and grow. Happiness, pleasure, and delight act as fuel for our spiritual being.

In a good sense, the food we yearn for symbolizes the pleasure or satisfaction of living a good life. Bread, for instance, represents a nurturing type of goodness and wholeness that feeds us. That is why we pray for our "daily bread." That is why Jesus called himself, "the bread which came down from heaven and gives life to the world." That is why bread is given in Communion. It represents the divine goodness and the heavenly delight that goodness brings.

On the other hand, the fleshpots of Egypt symbolize a delight that is far from heavenly. Longing for the fleshpots of Egypt is as bad as it sounds. It symbolizes longing for sensual pleasure apart from what is spiritual. This food represents the infernal delight received from acts of selfishness, evil and disorder. For example, the fleshpots may represent the raw appetite for sexual pleasure apart from love; or the burning sense of satisfaction from hatred, criticism, or revenge; or the sense of inner inebriation of an inflated ego drunk with pride; or the thrill of power when manipulating others. The fleshpots of Egypt symbolize the pleasure of human evil. When in a time of spiritual hunger for satisfaction in life, we may be tempted by a longing to return to the pleasure of destructive ways. The hunger is real. How we satisfy it is the problem.

When we first leave the delight of a sensual life behind, we don't immediately substitute the delight of a spiritual life. At first we experience a void between the two, between Egypt and Canaan, between the fleshpots and the milk and honey. We are tempted to look back and hunger for the pleasures we used to feel.

For example, the young man who left a life of sexual promiscuity and disorder for a loving and responsible relationship with one woman may begin to remember and long for the "good old days." Perhaps he has been married for five or six years and he enters a time when his sexual relationship with his wife doesn't feel fulfilling. It's tolerable, but not as wild and exciting as those "fleshpot days" of his youth. He fantasizes about being in college again, or being single, and hitting the bars, the parties, picking and choosing a new savory piece of flesh to satisfy him each night and discarding the leftovers in the morning. He longs for that promiscuous life again or for some other partner to fulfill his sexual drive. He hungers for the fleshpots of Egypt.

In another example, Jessica may not have lived a wild sexual life before marriage, but may begin to long for the freedom she used to enjoy when she was single. Not that her single life was a sinful life, but the hunger of a married person longing for a previous state can be a destructive hunger for the fleshpots. One can become blind about married life but be even more blinded by fond thoughts about the way things used to be. For instance, Jessica may tire of arguing, tire of her daily search for love and forgiveness, tire of being responsible, friendly, and compassionate in her wilderness of a marriage. So she may begin to recall her past. She fondly remembers being single, when she could do what she wanted any time she wanted to do it, when life was carefree and simple, self-serving, and self-oriented. She might inwardly say, "I wish I were back in the life I used to lead, when I could do what I wanted and no one bothered me. Why have I been caught in this trap? If I don't get out of this relationship, I think I'm going to die."

There are times to end relationships, but I have counseled several people like Jessica who are tempted to give up the journey of marriage right when things get a little dry and the real growth is about to start. They have to give up the fantasy that the good old days were better and focus on the real potential for growth in the future in what may be a temporarily challenged but potentially rewarding relationship.

How many people have escaped addiction or compulsion only to find themselves in a vacuum of delight for a while? Perhaps the alcoholic man has lived without a drink for six months and has felt the bonds of addiction lift. But following the initial freedom and consolation, he senses an emptiness inside. He has worked to find new methods to cope with life, new places to find happiness, new activities to fill his time, new, healthier friendships. But he doesn't feel he has arrived. He begins to look back at his drinking days with fond memories. Sure, back then he was under the dominion of the bottle, but the euphoria after that first drink was extraordinary! It made him feel so good, so happy, so content with life. Nothing makes him feel so important, so godlike anymore. And he misses the bars, the camaraderie of his drinking buddies, the wine, women, song. He, like the children of Israel, might say to his God, "Why did you lead me to this feeling of emptiness in my life, to die an unhappy and sober man? It would have been better if I had died an alcoholic. At least then I'd die with a smile on my face. I remember sitting there at the bar drinking as much as I wanted. . . . Where have those days gone?"

Most recovering alcoholics recognize that those days were days of bondage. Nevertheless, from time to time, we all long for the good old days back in Egypt because we, even like the Israelites, forget the realities of life back there. Certainly, we ate all the flesh we desired, but we often paid for it with slave labor, with personal plagues, and with loss.

The children of Israel couldn't return to Egypt. Imagine if they had assembled a group to go back. First of all, it's highly doubtful that the Red Sea would part for them this time. Spiritually, the Divine wouldn't perform miracles to lead them back into the bondage they had just escaped. If Israel really wanted to get back to Egypt, and if they took the same route, they'd have to swim. Even if they could cross the Red Sea to return, what would have happened to them when they returned? I doubt pharaoh would come forth with a large greeting party, put his arm around their shoulders and say, "Welcome back to Egypt! We've missed you so much. Make yourselves at home!" He may have done that, and then turned them around and slit their throats. And if pharaoh didn't kill them, surely, he would have returned them to exactly the same life of bondage, slavery, and death.

Spiritually, we can't really go back to Egypt. If we thought honestly about it, we wouldn't want to anyway. But we can, unfortunately, let ourselves forget the bondage and all the pain it carried with it. We remember only the brief moments of sensual satisfaction. The young man who longs for the days of promiscuity has forgotten about the bondage of those days: how he could never satisfy his hunger for the flesh, which grew into a cruel and taunting taskmaster; how he felt empty and unloved, guilty for tampering with and using others' emotions. The wife who longs for the "independence" of single life forgets the emptiness and loneliness she felt. She forgets her desire to escape that sense of isolation and self-indulgence. She doesn't permit herself to think about the consequences of leaving her marriage: the painful destruction of the relationship, the hurt and confusion inflicted upon the children, the guilt and emptiness after it's all over. The alcoholic vividly remembers the fleeting moment of euphoria, the few drunken good times. But he forgets the pervasive sense of guilt and self-condemnation. He forgets the hangovers, the blackouts, the myriads of broken bot-

tles, windshields, promises, relationships, lives. It is easy to forget
the bad times, but they are real.

I know that this longing is real, not only from personal experience, but also because I have counseled many alcoholics. I have also
counseled men and women trying to escape sexual addiction, as
well as others coping with marital challenges. The desire for an easy
way out—of avoiding the work that produces growth—is great.
The temptation to go back to old ways is something that you will
face if you are taking the spiritual journey. When in this state
between hell and heaven, Egypt and Canaan, when there's a void
of delight in your life, you will find yourself longing for the "good
old days." It is essential, at those times, to confront your inward
self. Get out in front of your inward self and grab your shoulders
with both hands, shake yourself a few times, look yourself right in
the eyes and shout, "Don't you remember the hell? You can't go
back there!" If that is just not your style, then perhaps you can simply console yourself with the knowledge that life does sometimes
feel empty, but, if you continue to trust in that higher power and
follow the right path, happiness will begin to fill the empty void.
For this is the truth. At first the happiness will be subtle, hardly perceptible, difficult to grab onto; but it will grow until it flows, even
as milk and honey, into your life.

Bread from Heaven

God did not abandon the children of Israel to starve in the
wilderness. After all, he had led them there. He wouldn't turn his
back on them before their journey's end. God told Moses that the
Israelites would be given food. They would eat bread every morning, and occasionally they would eat quail in the evening. Both
foods symbolize pleasures or spiritual delights that the Divine
offers us during our time in the wilderness.

One morning, the children of Israel awakened to find white stuff
lying all over the ground—small, round flakes, as fine as frost.

It tasted a bit like honey wafers, we are told, but the Israelites didn't discover that right away because they didn't immediately pick up this stuff and eat it. In fact, they couldn't even identify it as edible at first. They asked, "manna?" *Manna* is Hebrew for "What is it?"—which makes the whole thing sound like an old Abbot and Costello routine. One person picked it up and said, "What is it?" Another came and noticed the stuff in his friend's hand and asked, "What is it?" The other replied, "Yes." And from there the whole camp became confused. Finally, Moses had to come out and tell them, "This is the bread that the Lord has given you to eat" (Exodus 16:15).

This bread from heaven symbolizes the heavenly bread the Divine feeds us. It can be called "spiritual delight." It is very delicate, fine as frost, faintly sweet, but quite a nourishing delight that the Divine gives us when we begin to grow spiritually. It is not an explosive, earth-shaking experience, but rather a faint sense of happiness, goodness, wholeness, and peace. It is called "manna" because in the beginning we don't recognize it for what it is. We can look for the great reward of living a spiritual life. We can look for heavenly choirs to sing our praises, for joy to drop into our laps. We can wait to be overwhelmed with inward tranquility and bliss, to be raptured, caught up to God, powerfully transformed in an instant of transcendental glory. But instead, at this time in our spiritual development, we receive only a slight, tender, barely perceptible (but quite real and substantial) sense of tranquility and bliss—a mild sense of serenity. Moses, or the guiding truth within us, has to tell us, "This is your daily bread. Eat it."

Although this bread is real and nourishing and does taste somewhat sweet in our mouths, it is not the milk and honey of Canaan that will begin to flow farther on down our spiritual road. The blossoming joy and happiness of Canaan still lie ahead in the promised land. Eventually, we will recognize tremendous blessings in our hearts, in our minds, and in our lives. During our search in the wilderness, the pleasure we receive from the growth we achieve is more like little flakes of bread than milk and honey. But they are just what we need during times of trial and temptation, so we ought to recognize this food and eat it. It is good for us, and it will support us on our journey.

Let's think for a moment about the various forms this spiritual manna takes in daily life. Perhaps you have sensed, during efforts toward spiritual growth, the peace that replaces worry when you decide to release it and let God take care of things. Or you may have sensed the sweetness that descends upon a relationship when you give a little bit extra to your partner or a loved one. Manna is the inner sense of self-worth you enjoy when you help or love another person. It is the sense of satisfaction after a job well done. It won't set the world on fire, but it is certainly wholesome, nourishing, and desirable.

Manna falls into our lives in so many ways. Some of the best times in my life have been when I have recognized the good things God has done for me. I appreciate the manna when I think of my family—my wife and four boys—and the pleasure of being surrounded by such love, innocence, and wonder. This is not to say that the boys can't be monsters at times, nor that Cathy and I don't have our fair share of contention. But the manna falls daily as the family journeys through this life together.

I can also sense the manna in my job and in the blessings it has brought me. Serving as a pastor has brought new and modest rewards each day. Manna is the sense of privilege I feel when I perform the work of the ministry, when I study, preach, teach, and lead people as best I can to a new understanding and awareness of their God. There is a lot of pain, a lot of failure, and a lot of thankless work in the ministry; but the delight is always there, ready to be received.

Manna falls for me in the simple acts of duty, in mowing the lawn, washing the dishes, fixing that window one of the children broke while hurling blocks at make-believe enemies, in disciplining kids who hurl blocks through windows trying to hit make-believe enemies. It falls as Cathy and I sit down to discuss how to improve our communication, trim the budget, or get out to have some fun together as a couple. It falls all the time. I have to recognize it. I have to pick it up and eat it—allow myself to receive this gentle delight—but it always waits for me each morning of my life. It's waiting there for all of us.

When I was a pastor in Chicago, Cathy had been active in feeding the homeless in that city's Uptown district. I remember well the first time her group drove in from the suburbs. I remember thinking that she probably felt a little apprehensive. I know I did. My wife was entering a new and unfamiliar situation in a somewhat dangerous neighborhood (the women were routinely escorted from their car to the shelter). But I was happy that she could find something she felt was a very useful act of charity that she could do regularly.

When she returned from this uncharted territory, I could see that she had found some manna in that place. She had a glow about her and a sense of peace. She said that she hadn't expected to get anything out of it for herself; but as she met and served these less fortunate people, she felt a sense of worth come over her that she had never experienced before. She had a new understanding of what it means to help people in need, and she had experienced how when one gives, one does also receive. She tasted a bit of the spiritual delight the Lord gives all of us when we do something good.

My friend Glenn teaches autistic children for a living. Because of his special abilities, he is given the children with the greatest disabilities and even the problem children. Once, when we were talking about some of the difficulties in life, he recounted the many episodes when one of his students would simply refuse to do even the most menial task, when a child objected to a suggestion and bit him on the arm, when another forgot to walk to the bathroom and soiled her clothes, when he has worked day after day to teach one new concept to a child who just doesn't break through.

I asked Glenn how he could possibly keep up his morale in a job like that. His face brightened, and I could see that he had been eating the manna in this wilderness at work. He said, "Because they need me. Because sometimes, just when I think I'm going to give up trying, the child does break through. And because every breakthrough brings them so much happiness. And that makes me happy too." That was his manna.

I'd like to recount just one more story. It doesn't really illustrate the spiritual benefit of actually doing something good, but of recognizing good. Sometimes manna can be found vicariously, in listening and sharing the happiness of others. Sometimes, as parents, or grandparents, we can eat of that manna as we see our children or our grandchildren grow up and enjoy the wonder and beauty of this world. One winter, just before Christmas, our seven-year-old son Jason was invited with his class to sing Christmas carols at a nursing home. His teacher had prepared the children by telling them that many of the people were very old. Some would not be able to sit up in their beds to listen or respond. She said, and correctly so, that some might not even be aware that the children were present, and not to worry about that, because their singing would still be very special to those who could listen.

Jason came home late for supper that evening after visiting the nursing home. I was eager to hear him describe it because he'd had limited contact with the very elderly. I was also curious to hear how the elderly had responded to these little carolers. I asked, "How did the caroling go, Jason?"

He hesitated for a moment of deep thought and wonder. Then he blushed, crossed his hands in front of him, smiled bashfully, and answered in a gentle voice, "Oh, it was fun."

He looked as if he were hiding something, some little treasure or secret, perhaps too special to share, even with his dad. But I had to find out. I asked, "Well, what was it like? Did the old folks like the music?"

He looked at the floor with a special smile that I cannot describe and confessed softly, "They cried."

"What did they do?" I asked, not quite understanding.

"They cried when we sang to them," he said with a look of both concern and pride. "And then they all wanted to touch us."

Tears filled my eyes. Manna was falling all around like the gentle snow that dropped to the ground outside our house that night.

Our daily manna can be anything from the good feelings that come from being useful and kind, to the satisfaction of doing your work well, to the inner delight that comes from loving and watching others grow. But we must recognize it, as it lies each morning all around us, and gather it each day, accept the delights that the Divine lays before us, receiving them into our lives as our daily bread. This is the bread that comes down from heaven and gives life to the world.

One Day at a Time

Moses instructed the children of Israel to gather only enough manna for each day. If they tried to keep the manna overnight (except the night before the Sabbath), it would spoil. They were supposed to take the bread that God had given them one day at a time. The children of Israel heard the warning; but did they obey? Are you kidding? They nodded their assent, waited till Moses turned his back, and then collected enough for a week or two! Typical! And as they had been warned, the next day the manna they had collected and stored turned rotten, stank, and became infested with worms.

The Israelites had to learn to live life one day at a time. How clearly that relates to our spiritual lives. God will give us our daily bread. The Divine will take care of us, give us that sense of goodness, pleasure, and well-being. To grab onto it, store it up, control it ourselves, bespeaks a mistrust of God, revealing doubt that the Divine will provide new bread each day. When the children of Israel collect that bread despite God's instructions, their action symbolizes our taking matters into our own hands, thinking we are in charge of the good that falls into our lives, thinking that we can control it, save it up, make our own happiness, rather than simply letting go and letting God daily rain down his bread from heaven for us.

Have you ever tried to hold onto the good times until they've turned rotten in your hands? I know I have. I tend to throw my whole ego into my work (no small feat, as it weighs a ton!) When work goes well, I'm OK. If not, I'm not. I have been working on this dysfunctional approach to life and improving it slowly, but it used to be a major problem for me. As I said before, early in my career, I started a new church congregation in the city of Chicago. During the struggle to build a self-sustaining church congregation, I had put far too much of my own self-esteem into the program. At one time I was even hospitalized for a "heart attack," which turned out to have been an anxiety attack instead. The attack was a clear warning that I should slow down, not invest myself so thoroughly in my work and not try to control the whole process.

The congregation outgrew the small restaurant where we met. We decided to move to a larger auditorium in a music school several miles away from our original site. The facilities were much better, adding room for a nursery, Sunday school, discussions, and other programs. Our move would be a risk: we might lose some church members who were attached to the old location, but it seemed to be the right decision. I promised myself not to end up in the hospital again. I decided consciously to let go and let God. We'd move; I wouldn't sweat it. If we succeeded, that would be fine; if not, God would still be around to pick up the pieces.

The move ran smoothly. In fact, that's when I began hoarding the manna. Some initial problems opened many new avenues for responsibility in this larger site. But people seemed to come out of the woodwork to volunteer for the new responsibilities. As we became settled in our new home, new visitors, new children, new programs, and more volunteers filled the church. Manna was falling everywhere.

Then I began to forget where the manna was coming from, or maybe more accurately, I wanted to make sure it didn't stop falling. So I began to jump in and control the situation. I collected that manna every Sunday, not only for myself but for every person in the entire church congregation. I had to satisfy myself that everybody was happy and that everybody had enough bread stuffed away to eat for a month in case of a sudden famine. I took it upon myself to greet every new visitor, to talk to them in depth, to make sure the regulars stayed happy too, to make sure the children got a good program, to make sure all were being fed. I furiously stuffed bags with manna, not trusting that God would continue to provide. You could find me downstairs with the custodians hauling up the books, offering table and lectern for the service. You could find me with the person in charge of chancel decoration checking that the flowers were beautifully placed beside the Bible. You could find me upstairs with the Sunday school teachers reviewing their lesson for that day. You could find me beside the book and pamphlet display making a few sales. You could find me in the kitchen filling the coffeemaker with a new batch of grounds for those sleepy-eyed parishioners of mine. And finally, you could find me where I was supposed to be, ranting and raving back and forth across the chancel floor, delivering the day's message with all the energy and gusto one human preacher could possibly muster, because these people had to get their daily bread, even if it killed me.

That's when the manna began to turn to worms. The worms became evident as I drove to church one Sunday with my hundred mental burdens, ready to dive in for another day of manna hoarding, when my chest tightened up so much that I had to pull the car to the side of the road. It wasn't a heart attack; it was the familiar pain of my anxiety attack two years earlier. Suddenly, as I crouched over the steering wheel, breathing in and out slowly, the kids in the back seat shouting and climbing on one another, wondering what Dad was doing, a light came on in my dense head. I heard Moses saying, "I told you only to collect enough for one day at a time!" I realized that I had slipped into a state of complete mistrust in God. I realized that I had begun to take his place by believing that I could somehow secure others' happiness, that I could control all things, satisfy all appetites, that I could provide manna for everyone in the camp. I released those bags of manna there in the car that morning. They're probably still lying on Armitage Avenue in Chicago. I promised myself to collect only enough for each day and to collect that bread only for myself. The Lord would assure that the others were fed.

I still encounter states when I am tempted to collect and hoard that manna. Most of us face this, in some facet, at some juncture, don't we? That's why God gave us the story. That's why his message is so clear. "Give us *this day* our daily bread," we are told to pray. "Do not worry about tomorrow, for tomorrow will worry about its own things. Sufficient for the day is its own trouble" (Matt. 6:34).

Quail in the Evening

The children of Israel received not only bread from heaven in the morning, but they also occasionally received quail in the evening. God recognized that they had become accustomed to the flesh of Egypt, so he obliged them with the flesh of the quail. Occasionally, at evening, quail were said to come up into the camp. The children of Israel caught them, prepared them, and ate them for supper.

Like manna, quail is also symbolic of delight or pleasure. If the manna symbolizes spiritual delight and the flesh of Egypt symbolizes sensual delight, what would the quail, a type of meat, symbolize? It too symbolizes a sensual delight, but one that brings reward for leading a loving and spiritual life. The meat of the quail symbolizes the natural delight we receive through a life of goodness and love.

This delight or pleasure does not rain down from above during the morning state of our lives. It is said to have occasionally "come up" (Exodus 16:13) into the camp. The spiritual delight comes from above, and the natural delight comes from below, from the senses. But both are necessary. In the morning of our lives, when we have a fresh attitude and perhaps some enlightenment about our spiritual destination, we can live on the tender feelings of happiness that we perceive within. But in the evening states of our lives, times when we are not so enthusiastic, when we have only a hazy picture of our spiritual destination, we need some pleasure to spur us on. We need to see and feel the worldly benefits that result from leading a spiritual life.

Manna is the slight perception of happiness that rewards us in the wilderness of life, and the quail symbolizes the outward pleasures we receive from leading such a life. These pleasures can stem from a variety of sources. For instance, when we begin to lead a loving and productive life, others will tend to like us more. We will make new friendships; we may find that people admire us and sometimes compliment us for the good work we do. The satisfactions we receive from these benefits are like the quail. We might begin to perform better at work; we might discover new interest in the business as we endeavor to grow spiritually. We may funnel this interest into a promotion, a raise, more money, more success. The pleasures we occasionally receive from these benefits are the quail.

The quail can also be the pleasant chemical reaction that our body produces when we show acts of love and do good things. The burst of energy in the heart when we break through our defenses and help another human being, the sense of physical warmth that loving can bring, and the excitement of becoming acquainted with someone more intimately are among the pleasures represented by the quail. They are the natural rewards we receive from doing good.

You may wonder whether it is wrong to enjoy such pleasures. After all, some churches often seem to teach the axiom "If it feels good, shun it." But this kind of pleasure is good and good for us.

God gave us the pleasures of the world to enjoy and has built rewards into the system. If you learn to love, to share, to help others, you cannot help but benefit. You receive these blessings from living a good life. As we read in Matthew 6:33, these blessings are "all the things that shall be added unto you," when you, "seek first the Kingdom of God."

Seeking the spiritual kingdom of God, and not simply focusing on the rewards of a loving, productive life, is really important. To seek pleasure by way of good deeds and insincere acts of love can bring on its own plagues.

Later on in the life of the children of Israel such a plague did befall them. They had wandered in the wilderness for many years, and their words reflect that, at least for a while, they weren't receiving the quail. They became tired of the manna. They complained to Moses, "Is there any way we can get some meat around here? We're tired of eating this bread every day! We want some meat to sink our teeth into" (see Numbers 11:16-35). At that point, God gave them a great flock of quail. They ate the meat; but even as they chewed it, God struck the camp with a plague that wiped out many of those who were eating.

This has a significant symbolic relationship to spiritual growth and development. People, like Israel, can grow tired of the simple pleasures a spiritual life can bring. They can choose to reject the spiritual delights and focus on the natural delights alone. But to crave the worldly delights a good life offers will bring its own spiritual plague.

For example, selfishness can motivate people to do good. Individuals can begin to act like more loving and charitable people than they truly are, not because doing good is the right thing to do but because it brings more friends. The desire for praise, rather than an honest desire to help someone in need, can motivate great acts of charity. "Success" in career can motivate people to work assiduously, while ignoring what is right or wrong or what is the most useful thing to do. These self-serving motives kill the essence of the spiritual growth process. Self-serving motives become a plague, because what might be done for spiritual gratification is done for the mere sensual pleasure. Suddenly, like the manna we tried to store up, the pleasure spoils. It turns rotten while still between the teeth and causes spiritual sickness.

Let one example suffice to illustrate how sick it is to focus in on that quail. Think of a loving hug between two people. The hug is an innocent and affectionate exchange between a teacher and a student. They feel warmth, sharing, even a brief feeling of unity in that simple hug. They are letting the Divine provide bread and quail. They are accepting the good pleasure that has come into their lives. Now, think of the hug again, but see this time that the teacher is not innocent or loving. The teacher is taking. In fact, the teacher is motivated by a desire to get as much of a physical kick as possible, sucking the life out of that student, under the pretext of a loving hug. We would even call that a form of sexual abuse. It's a sick image and rightly so. That's an example of taking the higher delight of a good act and focusing on the worldly delight alone. It fast turns rotten and breeds worms.

Early in our spiritual growth we will hunger for occasional meat. Although perhaps not as dysfunctional as the teacher just mentioned, we may gently push away the manna and turn to the quail alone for delight. Especially in the beginning, we will work from mixed motives. We will want both the spiritual and the natural delight in leading a good life. And that is fine. God provides both the bread and the quail, but on his terms, not ours. He gives us what is good for us. He gives us what we need for that day. He knows what we need and he provides. We must learn to accept this divine guidance and accept what is given to us one day at a time.

Remembrance

The last notable event in this story of the manna is that God commands Israel to save some manna in a container for remembrance. He instructs the Israelites to show it to future generations as a memorial of how he cared for them in the wilderness. This manna did not spoil. It lasted for forty years or more. That is because this incident of storing manna symbolizes not hoarding or saving up because we are afraid to deplete our supply of good times. This bread is for remembrance. God urges us to remember what he has done for us, to remember his goodness and loving care. This is the same message that Christians receive in the New Testament from Christ himself. Jesus, lifting the bread of the Passover, said to his disciples, "Do this in remembrance of me" (Luke 22:19).

The Divine wants us to remember, to remember how we were cared for in those years of wandering. God did not abandon us. He filled each one of our empty days and wilderness nights with meaning. Every morning we awoke to some spiritual delight, and every night we enjoyed a good meal of natural satisfaction and pleasure in following the divine will.

Exercises

1. Ask yourself, "What destructive pursuits of pleasure prevent me from receiving genuine happiness? Do I have my own personal fleshpots?" If so, begin some decisive steps to leave them behind.

2. Do you know how to have fun? Experiment by looking for a new hobby or form of recreation: jogging, bowling, crocheting, writing, painting, walking, etc. Find a useful means of recreation to incorporate into your life.

3. What little pleasures do you get out of life? Do you ever reward yourself? In the next couple of days, go out and do something good for yourself. Remember: it must be something good!

4. When you feel empty and spiritually hungry for happiness in your life, pray, "Give us this day our daily bread. Help me to recognize this bread in my life."

Then all the congregation of the children of Israel set out on their journey from the Wilderness of Sin, according to the commandment of the Lord, and camped in Rephidim; but there was no water for the people to drink. Therefore the people contended with Moses, and said, "Give us water, that we may drink." And Moses said to them, "Why do you contend with me? Why do you tempt the Lord?" And the people thirsted there for water, and the people murmured against Moses, and said, "Why is it you have brought us up out of Egypt, to kill us and our children and our livestock with thirst?" So Moses cried out to the Lord, saying, 'What shall I do with this people? They are almost ready to stone me!" And the Lord said to Moses, "Go on before the people, and take with you some of the elders of Israel. Also take in your hand your rod with which you struck the river, and go. Behold, I will stand before you there on the rock in Horeb; and you shall strike the rock, and water will come out of it, that the people may drink." And Moses did so in the sight of the elders of Israel.   Exodus 17:1-7

CHAPTER FIVE

Refreshing Insights

Water from a Rock

The waters that flowed forth from the rock symbolize divine truth, and the people drinking of them symbolizes spiritual nourishment.

Apocalypse Explained 411:5

Is God with Us or Not?

Have you ever noticed that when things go wrong you wonder why your life is *always* so miserable? Have you ever noticed that when you feel depressed you can't think of one good thing that has ever happened to you and the future looks just as bleak? Have you ever felt in times of spiritual temptation that you haven't moved forward an inch in your spiritual growth, that you seem to be just where you were two years ago? Why does that happen to us? We can be progressing very well in our spiritual growth and development when suddenly something bogs down, one thing or another begins to go wrong, and we wonder to ourselves, "Is God with us or not?"

Two stories related to me serve well as fairly typical examples of how things can seem to go wrong and cause us to doubt the validity of the path we have chosen and to question whether God is with us or not.

Tim had been working hard to learn to let go and let God. He had been working with adult-children-of-alcoholics issues, and the strongest of these was learning not to worry and try to control every aspect of his life. He was making real progress taking life one day at a time. He had made a consistent effort to pray to God each morning for guidance. He slowly learned not to worry so much about his bills; he realized that worrying about them wouldn't pay them. He also made a decent effort, with some success, to slow down at work. He finally came to see that he didn't have to be the workaholic he used to be, that he wouldn't be fired if he relaxed occasionally, for a change. Tim's new state of letting go brought him some peace. He just began to realize, "Maybe life can be a safe place. All that worrying I used to do was a waste."

But as soon as Tim began to feel comfortable about life, the furnace broke down. A repairman recommended that Tim buy a new one. "How am I going to afford that?" he wondered. His phone soon rang, and it was St. Francis Hospital, informing him that, since he had not paid the bill for the tests he took three months ago, they would submit his name to a collection agency. He argued with them, hung up, and said to himself, "That's crazy! I submitted those claims to the insurance company about a week after the tests!" He called the insurance company and, of course, there was no answer. He grabbed his keys, jumped in the car, which curiously had trouble starting, and headed to the office to catch up on some work. But this brief journey confirmed that life had somehow turned against him. A car screamed through a red light, almost taking off the front end of his Volkswagen. Then, a truck cut him off on the highway; if he hadn't hit the brakes at that very moment, he would have been flattened. He pulled into work shaking, angry, indignant, saying, "I didn't ask for this! What do you want from me, God? I've tried to give it over to you and what happens? My life falls apart! Are you on my side or not?" He felt that God had abandoned him and all his efforts to let go had been in vain. It seemed right then that either God was a cruel practical joker, or perhaps there was no God at all.

Another example of a time when things seemed to go wrong just when they were beginning to go right happened to Mitch and Janis, who had been married for eight years and experienced a lot of growth together. But two years ago they had hit bottom in their marriage, and even wondered if their relationship would ever survive. Their terrible communication problems led them into a pattern of verbally shooting first and asking questions later. One time Mitch left for a week because the loud and vicious arguing was beginning to affect the children negatively. But Mitch and Janis worked with a counselor for a year and a half, developing a new respect for and understanding of each other. Over the following year they grew together as a couple, and learned to rely not just on themselves but on basic spiritual principles in their marriage: commitment, charity, trust, and faith in a higher power. They learned to live together and to love. In fact, they had enjoyed six months without a single violent explosion of temper. They had several arguments, but they had learned to handle them with more understanding and to back off when necessary. They had learned to make up. Marriage became something good for Mitch and Janis. They were not just on peaceful terms but on loving terms. They felt truly in love.

But one day Mitch received a call from an old girlfriend who had moved into town; she wanted to get together with him to talk over old times. Mitch asked Janis about this. Janis basically replied, "Over my dead body." Mitch tactfully declined his former girlfriend's invitation. But less than a week had passed before his former girlfriend called again. This time, Janis answered the phone. The girlfriend's few vague statements to Janis subtly indicated that her affection for Mitch had never completely died and that, perhaps, the same might be true of him. Apparently, the same was not at all true of him; nevertheless, Janis began to lose the new trust she had developed for Mitch. One Sunday, before dinner, she accused him of not loving her. He became indignant and sprang back with accusations of control and manipulation. Janis shot back that she wouldn't be that way if he wasn't so untrustworthy. Mitch said maybe he should have married his ex-girlfriend because at least she showed some real affection toward him. Their argument went on, spiraling downward into more and more vicious confrontation. They took a break for the night, exhausted from the battle; but it continued the next day, on the phone while he was at work, and later, over supper, and that night, and into the next day.

In recounting the story they confessed that at one point, each in his or her own way wondered, "How could this happen? It seems as if we're back where we were two years ago. All that work and nothing has changed. It's the same old thing. This marriage isn't going anywhere. Is this marriage supposed to be or not?" They both felt frustrated and confused. They needed answers, and they were definitely angry at each other and at life in general. We will return to these people and how they got back on track later in this chapter.

Unlike the people in the stories above, while we are on our spiritual journey, we don't necessarily have to have some unfortunate circumstance come along to knock us off our moorings. Sometimes we just begin to feel like we're in a rut for no reason at all. Sometimes, when it comes to our spiritual growth, we can wake up one morning and feel as though we've been abandoned. We feel alone, lacking something but we don't know what it is. We don't seem to have the same base or foundation we used to have. We feel uneasy, confused, thirsting for answers again. We may wake up in our own comfortable bed where we've slept for years, but find ourselves mumbling the lyrics of an old song by the Talking Heads, "This is not my beautiful house. This is not my beautiful wife. . . . How did I get here?"

Similarly, we can also fall into temptations to return to old ways of life without any provocation. We may wake up with an urge to smoke or drink, after having quit for five years. We may find we have a temptation to fantasize about our own importance or about sexual situations we used to wish we were involved in, even though we had supposedly abandoned this thought pattern years ago. We find ourselves in the wilderness again, thirsting, and wondering whether God is with us, and if so, why he doesn't take care of us.

This happened to the Israelites. They found themselves feeling as if they had made no progress in their journey across the wilderness. They found themselves thirsting again. This time there were no waters of Marah, though, to console them. They looked around and saw only rocks, a shrub or two, dirt, and dust. They cried out to Moses for water. They murmured and complained in anger. "Is God with us or not?" they asked indignantly (Exodus 17:7).

"Is God with us or not?" That's a curious question for these people to ask. No wonder Moses, after hearing their murmuring, replied, "Why do you tempt the Lord?" (Exodus 17:2). Moses was wondering why God didn't just strike them dead right there after all he had done for them. But, of course, he wouldn't do that. God is love. After seeing how patient God was with the children of Israel, and with our very selves, we can understand that God truly is all loving, forgiving, and by all means, patient.

"Is God with us or not?" How easily Israel had forgotten. Was he with them when the Red Sea had split in two, saving them from their oppressors? Was he there when they threw the wood into the waters of Marah, making those waters sweet? Had he not given them bread each day of their lives and led them safely through the wilderness? The answer is a loud and hearty "YES!" Yes, he was there every time they whimpered and cried. He comforted them, fed them, gave them water, protected them from harm. And he is there with them at every point of the journey if they'd only stop their complaining and listen to him. The new and fresh water that they need to sustain them is lying concealed, perhaps, all around them. They need only listen to learn how to see it and use it to bring their lives sustenance.

It seems almost bizarre that the Israelites would so quickly forget about their God. But it's not surprising, when we view this story as an allegory of our spiritual journey. For we do exactly the same thing when trouble occurs. Like Tim and Mitch and Janis, we forget the good things the Divine has done for us, the changes and progress we have made, the real miracles we have experienced in our lives. We focus on the very moment, and wonder whether we've made any progress at all on our spiritual journey. We may doubt that God has ever been with us or that he ever will be.

In Tim's story, he had forgotten the anxiety and fear he used to feel before he allowed a power greater than self to lead him. Certainly, his external life had become rough that day; but many miracles had occurred prior to this rough time, and he was a different person. If Tim were to stop complaining and evaluate, he would recognize his great spiritual strides. Of course, God had not abandoned him and was with him even then. In fact, if Tim only concentrated on his progress and the new ways of coping that he had worked to develop, he would begin to feel a lot better a lot sooner. Rather than seeing a hopeless situation in which anxiety and fear can come swooping back down into his life, Tim had to recognize the potential for strength and growth that were his for the asking. But he had to recognize it and tap into it.

The same is true with Mitch and Janis. They could become very distraught, wondering why they had relapsed, why their relationship had gone nowhere but down. But it hadn't. This wilderness of thirst and turmoil seemed to be their only reality, but it was only a temporary setback. They seemed to have gotten nowhere, and God seemed not to be with them. But in reality, God was still with them. The answers they needed for support and progress were within reach, waiting to be recognized and used. It was up to them to tap into those answers and find the truth that would help them.

Tapping into the Rocks

The children of Israel may have felt that they hadn't made much progress since leaving Marah and Elim. They had traveled far to a land that may have looked familiar but was actually very different. They encountered a more mountainous and rocky region as they traveled toward Mt. Sinai, but that was not its only difference. There was something magical about that place. No pools of water

lay nearby as in Marah, no palm trees and wells as in Elim; nevertheless, the most refreshing water yet was about to gush forth into
their lives from the strangest of places. God would provide, and
they would drink. Moses was told to lead the elders of Israel to the
rock at Horeb. He was commanded to strike the rock with his rod,
entreating God to bring forth water from it. He did so, and clear,
cool, spring water came gushing out. All of Israel celebrated and
saturated themselves in the newfound refreshment.

When it comes to our spiritual lives, Moses' tapping that rock
symbolizes our tapping into the knowledge we have, in times of
spiritual thirst and temptation. It means using the ideas, facts, and
bits of knowledge, which we have encountered in our spiritual
quest to help us through times of turmoil. It means finding the living truth in the rocks that surround us in our conscious minds.

You might say, "What? Rocks symbolize knowledge, facts,
ideas? If you think I'll believe that you must think I have rocks in
my head."

My reply would be, "Well, Yes. You do. At least I hope you do.
And you better start finding out how to tap into the truth of that
knowledge if you want to be refreshed in times of spiritual turmoil."

Rocks really do symbolize factual knowledge, especially knowledge about spiritual life and faith. Think of how rocks are used in
the Bible as symbols of what we know and believe.

In Matthew 16:18, we find that Jesus, finishing his sermon on the
mount, said, "Whoever hears these sayings of mine, and does
them, I will liken him to a wise man who built his house on the rock;
and the rain descended, the floods came, and the winds blew and
beat on the house; and it did not fall, for it was founded on the
rock." He was saying that those who build their life on the firm
foundation of the divine truth would endure any period of spiritual turmoil. Christ urged his disciples to build on the knowledge
of the spiritual life he had described.

Later in the gospel of Matthew, Jesus asks his disciples, "Who
do the people say that I am?" Peter answered, "You are the Christ,

the son of the living God." Jesus said, "Blessed are you Simon Bar-Jonah, for flesh and blood has not revealed this to you. . . . And I also say to you that you are Peter, and on this rock I will build my church, and the gates of hell shall not prevail against it." Jesus was actually using a play on words. "Peter" in Greek is *Petros*. The word for rock in Greek is *petra*. Jesus was saying, "Petros, your new name is Petra [Rock]. And upon this petra I will build my church." What does this mean? Why was Peter the rock? Why would his words become the foundation of the church? Peter had professed that Jesus was, indeed, the Christ. This tenet of faith became the foundation upon which Christianity was founded. For Christians, the rock of Christianity is the belief that Jesus is the Christ.

In relation to that, Jesus quoted an old prophecy, from Psalm 118:22, 23, that had come true with his coming: "The stone which the builders rejected has become the chief corner stone. This was the Lord's doing, and it is marvelous in our eyes" (Matthew 21:42). The stone symbolizes the knowledge or belief that Jesus is the Messiah. The builders who rejected that stone were the scribes and pharisees. Jesus was saying, through the symbolism of ancient parables, that one knowledge or belief, rejected by the leadership of the prevailing church at that time, eventually would become the chief cornerstone or most important knowledge of faith for the Christian church.

In many instances in the Old Testament stones or rocks symbolize knowledge or beliefs. The writer of Psalm 61:2 asks God so eloquently, "Lead me to the rock that is higher than I." This, in spiritual terms, means, "Lead me to a greater understanding or knowledge than what I have now."

Many are familiar with the story of the young David who slew the giant Goliath. David, in slaying Goliath, picks five smooth stones out of the brook to hurl at the monster and bring him to destruction. Goliath symbolizes a giant problem or character defect

in a person's spiritual life. If an individual selects the right knowledge, or stone, out of the flowing brook, God's Word (in whatever way he or she sees it), and uses it in life to counteract that
problem, the spiritual giant will be defeated. The simple, smooth,
well-worn facts about the spiritual life are always the best defense
against an opposing spiritual foe, no matter how overwhelming
in size.

Observe how stones are used in architecture. One use is to build
foundations. Don't we build our life on our knowledge and beliefs?
Rocks or stones can be placed on one another to build walls. In a
good sense, these would represent whole doctrines of thought used
to build great mental structures, skyscrapers, towers, walls of protection. In a bad sense, as in the story of Jericho, which is coming
up later in this adventure, the walls represent knowledge or ideas
piled up on one another to protect something hurtful. These walls
can represent excuses and denials.

Rocks, stones, boulders, and the like represent knowledge, facts,
things known. Knowledge exists all around us in this wilderness
journey. We encounter so many facts. But not all of them grab our
attention or seem to be of much use. For instance, how much
knowledge from school do you really use? Much of it just sits there
stone-dead, useless, until called upon. This is just as true for the
knowledge we have about leading a spiritual life. Like Israel passing through the mountainous terrain, we hardly notice the rocks
that surround us. But facts are facts, no matter what the subject; and
they may be important to us when we least expect it. A rock is a
rock, an inanimate object—that is, until it is used. Until, as in this
story, it is tapped into.

Now, before learning how to tap into these rocks, it might be
valuable to identify the rocks that lie there lifeless in your life.
Perhaps as you imagine yourself in the wilderness, you can recognize one or two. One rock, or knowledge, may be "God is love."
That's a big rock, isn't it? But what does it mean? Those three

words sound really good together, but can you find living truth within that statement? Can water come out of that rock?

Another rock, perhaps not as heavy as the first, might be, "Let go and let God." Pick that one up and examine it for a while. Is it a significant statement, or is it just another empty phrase to stumble over or repeat in a twelve-step meeting each week?

What about, "Do unto others as you would have them do to you"? You've seen that rock appear here and there in the wilderness since you were young. In fact, you remember that one from when you wandered the land of Canaan as a child. But what does it mean now? Is it relevant to your life? Can you squeeze some water out of that stone? What rocks lie around in your life, ready to be tapped into? It's an important question.

How do we tap into those rocks? Moses is told to take his rod and strike at the rock of Horeb, entreating God to bring water out of it. Now, we could analyze this same wooden rod being used the way the wood was used at the waters of Marah. Similarities exist. But some questions can be left for the inquiring theologians to ponder. What is important to our spiritual growth is that these dead facts will not come alive and help us unless they are approached with great urgency. We must find that knowledge or belief that would help our particular condition and ponder it, hammer on it for an answer, ask God to bring forth the living truth from it, so that it may bring us relief.

This process can be understood more clearly when we imagine the biblical story itself. Imagine Moses, in front of all the elders of Israel, standing before the rock of Horeb. What did he think or say? Maybe he thought or said something like this: "O God, I have found this great rock you have told me would help in this time of strife. I know it can help, for you have led me to it. I cannot understand how or why; but I will strike this rock with my rod, as you have commanded, and ask you to bring life from it for me and my people."

Maybe at that point he strikes the rock. Maybe water comes out immediately. Maybe nothing happens. Maybe he strikes it more than once, beseeching God to bring forth the water, asking to see the water come forth, begging to feel its life-giving flow. And finally, the water begins to flow until soon it is gushing forth like a geyser and all the elders of Israel begin to dance under its soothing stream like children playing under a fountain.

What Moses did is what we must do when we thirst for new truth, when we experience a time of turmoil or spiritual crisis. Where is the rock to which God is trying to lead us? What dead knowledge can come alive for us in this time of distress and bring relief? Perhaps this rock is a quotation from the Bible, maybe a simple saying from a self-help program, perhaps a technique learned in therapy. Whatever it is, we find it as we rummage through our minds. We, like Moses, don't know exactly how it all works or why, but we ask God to bring forth truth from that knowledge. We urgently ask him to help us. We hit that rock. We meditate on it. We cry over it. We pray to God to allow the truth to flow forth from this dead factual information. And suddenly it begins to come alive and brings relief.

As we take that truth in and live by it, the rock begins to gush forth even more. Soon, a new understanding begins to reveal itself to us. We see that we are not doomed to feel empty and spiritually depleted. Soon, we begin to see that we have made real progress in life, that we won't die in this temporary state of distress, and that God is certainly with us. But to prompt this change we had to take what knowledge we had about our situation, no matter how dead or useless it seemed to be at the time, and strike at it with great force, praying to God to allow the truth to come flowing out.

And so we return to Tim, who was fast becoming anxious over life again. What must he do? He had to listen to the voice of God, leading him to the rock or knowledge that would help him in his time of need. For Tim, the rock was the Serenity Prayer. He had used it before, and felt some comfort from it. He decided to use it again. This time though, he wondered if it would bring relief. But a faint voice within, actually more of a feeling, told him, even as it

told Moses, "Go to this rock. I will stand there before you." Tim
began to bring the prayer to mind. He stopped all his work at his
desk, turned to the window, and recited the prayer to himself.

"God, grant me the serenity to accept the things I cannot change;
the courage to change the things I can; and the wisdom to know the
difference."

After that Tim said the prayer again, and again, asking God to make
its meaning come alive, to release the truth and wash away his hot
anxiety and fear. He pondered each sentence. He concentrated on
the word "serenity." He wondered, "What does it mean? What
does it mean in my life? God! Yes, *God* grant me serenity. I know I
can't grant it myself. Courage . . . now that's a word! And wisdom?
I know nothing."

Tim allowed himself these thoughts for a while, and he tapped
on that rock by repeating the prayer again and again. Soon the
water did begin to flow. He suddenly remembered saying that
prayer in a large group of twelve-steppers. As this memory bub-
bled up into his consciousness, he instantly felt their support; he was
not alone. He remembered talking to another member about fear,
and he recalled that the other person had learned to turn her own
similar fears over to God. "God," he said to himself, "There's God
again." He began to think as he sat in his office chair, "It really is
God, and not me, who runs this show. God can give me serenity,
even as the prayer says. Hey, I've seen that before. As long as I keep
giving the control back to God, he takes care of it. Remember when
I had that car accident? I turned it over then, even if it was the other
guy's fault. At least I didn't have an accident today! What's the big
deal? I don't know how I am going to pay for this furnace, but I
could try that insurance company again about those bills. After all,
the prayer says, 'Give me the courage to change the things I can.'
And this is one of those 'things'."

The water had begun to flow for Tim. It may not have come
gushing out all at once. It took Tim a few hours to extract enough

sustenance from that rock to carry on; but he did find relief, and the crisis became manageable, and under control—not his control, but the control of someone a lot more powerful and a lot wiser than Tim.

Mitch and Janis also had to go to the rock, or in their case, several rocks. They had been counseled. They knew that they shouldn't punctuate their arguments with accusatory statements. They knew which buttons to push if they wanted to provoke their spouse. Mitch knew that Janis needed reassurance because she tended to be insecure. He saw that rock lying there in the wilderness. He didn't like it, but he saw it. Janis knew that if she would only take one step backwards and apologize for calling him names, Mitch would do the same. She saw that rock lying there. She had been ignoring that rock intermittently through eight years of marriage.

Mitch and Janis had to begin to recognize that they were being called to the rock, whatever that knowledge may be, and they had to bring out the truth in that knowledge. Janis had to acknowledge that Mitch really did demonstrate love and commitment in the past year. She had to stand before that knowledge and pray to God to allow her to see the truth in it, to experience the truth that she is loved. Janis asked God to bring forth the water from that rock. It eventually came forth. As soon as she really meditated on it, tried hard to understand it, she began to experience Mitch's love, and to feel that she was lovable. But Mitch also had to come to see the fact that sometimes he did, in his own words, "act like a jerk," and that Janis still needed reassurance that his days of non-commitment and casual love were over. Mitch faced that knowledge and prayed to God to help him feel its truth come forth, so that he could get back on his own track. He wanted to feel a bit more responsibility and compassion, and allow healing to begin. The water began to flow.

Mitch and Janis are still together and growing as a couple. Tim is still coping with life, and living with a lot less fear and a lot more peace of mind than he used to. (By the way, the local oil company gave him an interest-free loan to pay for his furnace, and the hospital finally received payment from his insurance company.) These people used what they had previously learned about life to help them in their challenging situations. They found the deeper truths within them and found nourishment by tapping into those truths.

In any situation of strife, there is knowledge that can help us. These rocks may seem like lifeless objects, especially when we are distracted by thirst and anxiety, but they can help. We need to find that knowledge, and like Moses, invoke the Divine with all our hearts to let the water flow, so that we can live, grow, and continue on our spiritual journey. If we do this, water will flow. In fact, if we teach ourselves to find and use the knowledge that lies dormant in our minds, it will become easier and easier to allow the water to flow out of whatever knowledge we choose. Statements like "God is love" and "Live and let live" or the Golden Rule and the Lord's Prayer, will take on new meaning, simply because we have approached these rocks and taken time to ponder them and ask God to reveal the living truth within them.

Only God Can Make Miracles

Some time after this first episode when water came forth from the rock, Moses was told to simply speak to the rock and it would produce water. He didn't have to hit it anymore. And the same is true with us. As we progress in our spiritual growth and development, we will learn to see a fact, knowledge, teaching, or a quotation from Sacred Scripture, simply focus on it, and easily perceive the truth within it without as much effort as we once needed. We will become increasingly sensitive to life in general, seeing not just the facts, but the truth that lies hidden within those facts.

But it is important to note that Moses did not obey God's second command, that he speak to, not strike, the rock. He brought all the people before the rock of Horeb and shouted to Israel, "Hear now, you rebels! Must we bring water for you out of this rock?" (Numbers 20:10). Then Moses hit the rock twice and water came out. God's response was a harsh one: He told Moses that he would not set foot into the promised land. He would lead the Israelites to that land, but not into it, because he had not hallowed God in front of Israel. He had taken credit for bringing the water forth, by claiming that he had the power, and he had hit the rock instead of speaking to it.

We might look at this story and wonder why God's response was so harsh. It doesn't seem so sinful that Moses said, "must *we* bring water?" Couldn't he take a little credit for at least being there to let it happen? And is it really that much of a sin that Moses hit the rock instead of speaking to it? Granted, he wasn't listening very well, and it seems he did believe that he could do it by himself, his way; but, still, the punishment seems unusually cruel.

Spiritually, when it comes to our inward journey, it does make sense that Moses couldn't enter the promised land. He had developed a belief that he did possess the power to bring truth from the rocks. And he appeared to do just that. But that was an appearance. God brought forth the water, even when Moses didn't acknowledge that a power greater than himself was the real miracle maker. God lets truth come forth in our lives too, if we tap into it, even if we don't acknowledge that it is the Divine who makes the water come forth. He'd rather have us find the truth and live it, thinking we produced it on our own, than have us die in the wilderness without it. But that does not mean that we shouldn't give credit where credit is due. And if we think believing that the power is ours rather than God's will lead us into the promised land, we are severely mistaken. That mind set must be left behind. We must accept that even the most noble part of our being has absolutely no power without God. We must come to see that we can't change ourselves, we can't part seas, we can't produce bread from heaven, we can't extract water from a rock. Only God can. We cooperate with God, we raise the rod, we throw the wood into the water, we collect the manna, we strike the rock—but we don't make the miracles happen. There is only one God; it's not Moses, nor is it we. It's God. As one of my best friends has said, "Maybe the problem is that we need to let God be God!" I have come to see that there is much wisdom in that funny statement.

The Wonder of Miracles

It would be easy to lose sight of the real miracles that occur as Israel journeys through the wilderness toward Canaan. The sheer number of miracles could distract the reader from focusing on each one of them. We could easily gloss right over them and miss the wonder and significance that they embody.

We can also gloss over the miracles in our own spiritual growth. For we do experience miracles, though we might not interpret them as such. We can experience the miracle of the rock of Horeb each day of our lives. Each new insight, each step forward toward what is right and good, each moment of love, compassion, and wonder can be seen, if we choose, as a miracle. We can be anywhere—at the supermarket, in our car, at work, at home in front of the television—and living water can burst forth into our lives, filling that one dry and empty moment with a bubbling spring. It can happen anywhere. It can happen anytime. It can happen often too, if we allow those miracles to enter our lives.

To close this chapter, I'd like to offer one instance of a little moment of wonder that I once experienced. This incident may sound trivial and a bit odd, because what I experienced were feelings, and feelings are difficult to describe. But my emotions brought a sense of refreshment and great joy and, after ample time for reflection, still seem to me to have been a brief flowing of water from a rock.

A few years ago I received a letter from my father about financial information I should file in the event of his death. My father loves to discuss that subject and to prepare me for it every time we get together. It's become one of his peculiarities. But his letter prompted me to consider life and death and unexpected changes. It seemed only a brief moment ago I was a child sitting on my father's lap, breathing in the scent of Old Spice aftershave mixed with the faint odor of Chesterfield cigarettes, listening to him sing a song about "Old Nelly with the wooden belly."

That image seemed like a dream. I reflected on my own fatherhood. How long would it be until my sons would grow to be my age and I my father's? I felt almost melancholy. Life seemed so short. I was just getting the hang of this father stuff and loving it. But in the blink of an eye my kids would be grown, and I'd be an old geezer, with no little one of my own to hold anymore.

Then, right on God's providential cue, my youngest boy waddled into the room and wanted me to pick him up. Steve was three years old, and the happiest, most pleasant toddler at times. I picked him up and put him on my knee, still in philosophical thought. I didn't sing to him "Old Nelly with the wooden belly," but I gave him a good long hug. I wondered how long I would be able to pick up my son like that and set him on my knee, because they get big, you know. It filled me with sadness to think about it. It really did, and bitterness, that life was so short. How many more times would I hold my son?

Suddenly, without conscious thought, I let the knowledge of "fatherhood" bring forth water. I closed my eyes and let it come. And it was released. In a flash flood I saw the truth of "fatherhood," that I was a father and a son, that God was a Father and we were his sons, that all three of us—my father, myself, and my son—were all brothers in the arms of eternity. About a million other realities about fatherhood flashed by as well. I not only saw it all; I felt it. It was a magnificent feeling of understanding; the knowledge of what it means to be a father seemed to embody new meaning and life. I also derived a deep feeling of comfort from these thoughts, that this moment of love between us, though a fleeting moment in this earthly realm, was something infinite and eternal in the eyes of God. I knew that we would always be together, somehow, some way, and that the question of how much longer I would be able to pick him up was only a question for this world.

Let me tell you, the waters flowed for me that moment. They didn't just flow figuratively, either. I stood up with my son in my arms while tears poured down my cheeks. He leaned back and looked at me so quizzically. I told him, "It's O.K. son. I'm just happy." He hugged me and patted me on the back, as if to say, "I understand Dad. I cry about things like that all the time."

Exercises

1. List the ways that you have experienced God in your life. Are there magical times of God's presence that you had forgotten about?

2. Every time you encounter a problem, ask yourself, "What are the facts to help me with this?" Search those facts for the living water within them that will help you solve the problem. Meditate on them. Learn from them. Use those rocks in your head.

Now the Amalekites came and fought with Israel in Rephidim. And Moses said to Joshua, "Choose us some men and go out, fight with Amalek. Tomorrow I will stand on the top of the hill with the rod of God in my hand." So Joshua did as Moses said to him, and fought with Amalek. And Moses, Aaron, and Hur went up to the top of the hill. And so it was, when Moses held up his hand, that Israel prevailed; and when he let down his hand, Amalek prevailed. But Moses' hands became heavy; so they took a stone and put it under him, and he sat on it. And Aaron and Hur supported his hands, one on one side, and the other on the other side; and his hands were steady until the going down of the sun. So Joshua defeated Amalek and his people with the edge of the sword. Then the Lord said to Moses, "Write this for a memorial in the book and recount it in the hearing of Joshua, that I will utterly blot out the remembrance of Amalek from under heaven." Exodus 17:8-14

CHAPTER SIX

Repelling Negative Thoughts

Amalekites

Amalekites in the Word mean falsities that attack truths.

Arcana Coelestia 5313

Spiritual Enemies

The children of Israel had known suffering. They had experienced the hunger and thirst that a life in the wilderness could bring. But they had not known war. In fact, if they had known, before they left Egypt, that they would fight one enemy after another before they could obtain the promised land, they probably would have decided to stay where they were. Perhaps that is why God didn't warn them. The children of Israel would fight enemies, not only to take the land of Canaan, but to protect themselves from harm as they journeyed toward Canaan.

Israel's enemies represent the enemies we encounter in our spiritual lives. Ours are not outward adversaries but inward adversaries. Our inward enemies take the form of character defects and destructive tendencies that begin to reveal themselves as we journey toward a better life. Sometimes our spiritual adversaries ambush us when we are vulnerable. At other times they boldly confront us and challenge us to fight against them and defeat them. And we must defeat them in order to find true peace and fulfillment in our lives and go on to inherit our own promised land.

But in order for these enemies to be confronted and defeated, they must be recognized. Many people are familiar with their own character defects. They remember well pharaoh and the plagues of Egypt, so they would not be surprised to find even more spiritual enemies hiding out there in the wilderness, ready to attack them. But not everyone has this awareness. Some leave the slavery of their own destructive tendencies behind and believe they will never face such powerful adversaries again. They wander the wilderness hungry and thirsty but quite ignorant of the dangerous character defects that lie deeply hidden within their unconscious. Like Israel, they wander the wilderness in hunger and in thirst, but initially encounter no enemies. They doubt that any such enemies even exist.

In teaching about spirituality, I have found that almost everyone can relate his or her life to the wilderness, but some people do not immediately recognize that within this desert wasteland lurk still more hidden and dangerous enemies. Many wander the wilderness without progressing to the point where they recognize the spiritual enemies within. There are, in truth, major destructive inclinations that emerge from time to time and strike people at their weakest point. But some people do not see that some major defects must be removed if they truly want a new way of life. The result is that some wander the wilderness their entire lives, never acknowledging their spiritual foes, never defeating these enemies, never entering the promised land of a new and beautiful spiritual life.

I recently encountered a woman at a twelve-step meeting who told the group that she really could not see any destructive tendency within herself. She said that upon serious reflection, she just could not label one particular aspect of herself a character defect or destructive tendency. She apologized to the group, intimating that this twelve-step program was not in touch with people's true spiritual nature. At the end of the meeting, as we were all still in a circle, she asked whether she could make just a few brief comments. This was unusual, but the group consented. She then singled out each person in the group and said "I know what's wrong with you, and with you, and you too!" She revealed to each person in the group exactly what she thought his or her problem was and gave each her solution to the problem as well. She truly believed that she didn't have any problems, but that everyone else in the room certainly did. Her own character defects were hidden from her because she was so busy finding defects in others.

To achieve real spiritual growth, you must recognize that you do possess certain harmful destructive tendencies. If you pay close attention to your thoughts, you will recognize these enemies as they sneak into your conscious mind and try to do damage. In fact, your first real spiritual enemies act like very calculating, sinister bandits, which rob you of your spiritual life and vitality. They are symbolized by Israel's first enemy, the Amalekites.

The Amalekites

As the Israelites journeyed into the mountains near Sinai, the Amalekites, a tribe of bandits, attacked them. This first battle was a surprise attack. We are simply told at this point in Exodus 17:8, "Now Amalek came and fought with Israel at Rephidim." We can imagine the Israelites' surprise. They had not known war before this time. Who were these Amalekites? They would soon learn more than perhaps they wanted to know. The Bible tells us that these Amalekites were cunning bandits who harassed the children of Israel as they made their way from Egypt to the promised land. Later on in their journey, Moses reminds the Israelites of the terrible days of Amalek: "Remember what Amalek did to you on the way as you were coming out of Egypt, how he met you on the way and attacked your rear ranks, all the stragglers at your rear, when you were tired and weary; and he did not fear God" (Deut. 25:17-19). This first ambush of Amalek may have been a head-on attack, but more likely it was one of these raids from the rear. We don't know for certain. But we do know that the Israelites were caught off-guard, and that these first spiritual enemies were ruthless, attacking when least expected, apparently upon "the rear ranks" and picking on the "the tired and weary" who were unable to protect themselves.

Specifically, the Amalekites represent inner spiritual bandits, the destructive thoughts that emerge from nowhere, often when we are down. They may surprise us. Just as we were hoping things would turn around for us, they attack us with thoughts of discouragement. Or when we become weak from our spiritual journey, they ambush us with a sense of loss and thoughts of hopelessness. These destructive thoughts attack our vulnerable spots, and they attack us from behind, when we least expect it.

These Amalekite-thoughts often hide in our unconscious and wait patiently until you and I are hurting and upset. They wait until we are weak and falling back from what we know is right. They wait until we begin to wander from the true path that we know we should take. Then suddenly they appear and pounce on us full strength. For instance, if you begin to feel depressed, they jump in to make you feel twice as depressed. If you begin to be afraid, they exploit it and try to turn your fear into terror. If you feel a bit guilty, they'll suddenly appear to turn your guilt into self-hatred. If you feel a twinge of dislike toward someone, they'll hasten you down the path of hatred and revenge. When the going gets tough, spiritually, the Amalekites get going. You can count on these destructive thoughts to emerge for a sneak attack, suddenly jumping out from behind the rocks and bushes of your spiritual wilderness, to beat you and steal the last of your healthy impulses, and then leave you for dead. These foes are determined.

Perhaps these Amalekites have sneak-attacked you? Have you ever been afraid of being left alone? Many have felt fear of abandonment. When, for instance, you are feeling insecure about your relationship with your spouse or partner, the Amalekites will always show up as soon as your fear begins to emerge. They'll meet you as you regress into states of fear and insecurity. They may begin by sounding supportive like a friend, but they slowly divert you from the right path and then begin their assault. They say, "Hey, Brad isn't exactly being very loving right now. That's truly scary, isn't it? You know, I wouldn't be surprised if he's up to something. Maybe he's moving away from you. Maybe he's been thinking about someone else. I wouldn't just keep up with the same old routine. If I were you, I'd start clinging to him right now! It's worked before. It'll work again. In fact, you start that coyness right away and lay that old guilt trip on him too, and don't forget the threat about leaving him. He always falls for that reverse psychology." Soon, the Amalekites can have you acting in the most destructive manner, playing out all your old tricks, telling all the old lies, clinging to your partner as tightly as you can: a great victory for these spiritual bandits.

The Amalekites can attack during an argument with your spouse or a loved one. Perhaps you are annoyed by one of those important issues of marriage—the "you've got to be kidding! Hamburgers again?" argument or the one about the proper way to squeeze toothpaste out of the tube. When you feel that you are losing the argument, you panic; you are losing the upper hand. You feel vulnerable and realize you must act decisively or your spouse will celebrate a clear victory. Suddenly, the Amalekites show up filled with words of advice. They say, "O.K. You're down. Now's the time. Remind her of what she did to you six years ago." They say, "Tell her she's just like her mother. You know how much she hates that. That'll put her on the defensive. Call her a few names. That always works!" The more you listen to these sneaky, destructive thoughts the more abusive they become. The more you follow their advice, the more abusive you become, and the greater is their victory over your spiritual life.

I am over it now and have become a nervous flyer rather than a fearful flyer, but the Amalekites often used to travel with me in an airplane. Now, I realize that almost everyone would say that he or she is a nervous flyer at times, but I had carried my anxiety to the point where I would almost sink into despair. I had beaten numerous compulsions and neurotic thinking in the past, especially through working in programs developed to help me with my spiritual growth. But the fear of flying was one of the last to go. Especially on a bumpy flight or during what was perceived to be an unusual procedure, my fear became terror. I knew all the safety statistics, but that did not help. I really became afraid. And when I did, the Amalekites emerged out of nowhere to help me. You might say that I let these nagging fears overcome my trust in God's providence.

I still prepare for takeoff by reading the little card to see where the nearest exit is in case we crash. In fact, that is what we are instructed to do by the flight attendant. The Amalekites used to show up at that time to tell me, "Look, who cares about the exit? You're going to be smashed into tiny bits and then burned to charcoal." I would laugh at the Amalekites' warning thinking to myself, "They really must take me for an idiot if they think that kind of blatant language scares me." I laughed, that is, until the plane would begin to take off. As the plane's engines roared and the huge and complex machine lifted off the ground, my heart would race and my hands sweat and cling to the armrests. The Amalekite, sounding as real as the passenger in the seat beside me, would lean over toward me and say, "It's amazing! How do these heavy things ever get off the ground?" Then he'd grin at me and say, "Well, actually, all of them don't! Remember the DC 10 that lost its engine at O'Hare? It crashed right down there. Hey! This is a DC 10! I wonder if the engine is securely bolted on? Why don't you look out the window and see?"

At that point, if I could even turn my head, I would follow his directions and look out the window at the engine on the wing. For some reason, when I fly DC 10s, I'm always seated right next to the engine. As soon as I could see the engine, the flaps would go down on the wing, and the plane lean drastically left and begin to spin into a sharp turn. I would ask myself, "What does this mean?" The

Amalekite would lean over to say, "Wow, this is unusual! I bet we're turning around to go back because of some mechanical failure. In fact, you see those flaps? I bet they're stuck like that. We're going to spiral here till we hit the ground!"

Usually, after we'd level off I'd relax. Once, however, after leveling off, I heard a noise that sounded like a crack in the fuselage. Before the Amalekite could speak I tightened my seat belt and thought, "Well, even if a hole does blow open in this plane, I'm safe now with my seat belt tightened." But that was before the accident over the Pacific, in which several passengers were sucked out of a hole, chairs and all. The Amalekites reminded me of that story every time I heard a strange sound in the wall beside me. They told me whatever would work to bring up my fears. If they could, they'd have me, dashing, in mid-flight, up the corridor to the cockpit screaming, "Open the door. I'm getting off right here!"

Although my recurring encounters with the Amalekites may sound humorous now, when I suffered from the fear of flying and was up in the air, they somehow didn't seem that funny. And that's true with most of our encounters with the Amalekites. They may start out by brazenly taunting us, but usually they end up being far from humorous.

The Amalekites can even lead us to harm ourselves or others. They often show up when we suffer from guilt, for instance. They introduce themselves as very caring friends, but then gradually twist their words and fill us with self-doubt and condemnation. They say, "Gee. I guess you feel pretty bad about what just happened, don't you? Well, do you really think you could help it? These things happen from time to time with most people, don't they? Well, maybe they don't. Maybe you are different. I guess most people aren't capable of acting like such a monster, are they? You probably don't even feel like a human being, do you? You're lower than a human being, aren't you? You don't deserve anything, do you? You don't deserve to feel good or happy. You really don't deserve to live. In fact, why don't you just kill yourself? It would be one way to rid the world of people like you, before you can do more damage." They'll continue as long as they can. In fact, if they can, they will take your life, if not literally, then figuratively, making you more and more miserable and unable to cope with normal pressures.

Destructive thoughts come into play in all phases of life. They are the little voices within, the cartoon devils on the shoulder, the Amalekites sneaking up at the back of the procession, to take us and lead us astray. They are the voices of fear, anger, jealousy, contempt, self-pity, guilt, lust, greed. The Amalekites are the thoughts that show up when we are down, to bring us to the ground, to rob us of the good we possess, to kill our joy and delight, and leave us barren, wasted, and half-dead. They will continue to ambush us every time we forget their presence, unless we act immediately. We must stop these thoughts, confront them once and for all, do battle against them. We must fight these Amalekites with what weapons we can find and call upon the Divine to work yet another miracle to rid us of these detestable malefactors.

Joshua: The Fighting Truth

The Amalekites had viciously attacked the Israelites. Moses and the children of Israel had to act to protect themselves. Moses appointed Joshua to be commander of the new Israelite army, and he asked him to select men for that army. In fact, Joshua would soon become the new leader of Israel, the man who would lead them into the promised land. But for the time being, he was told to take his army out in the morning and do battle with these new enemies. Moses promised that he would stand on the top of the hill with his rod in his hand, to call upon God for strength, for miracles, and for victory.

Joshua, who was chosen to be the one to vanquish this foe, represents a certain kind of truth within us that leads us to conquer our spiritual foes. Moses represented a type of truth called "the law," and Joshua represents a type of truth that we may call "fighting truth." Joshua is called upon to battle the enemy. Eventually he will lead us to conquer the spiritual foes who prevent us from fully enjoying life in the promised land. The fighting truth is what cuts through all the false ideas that have hurt us and held us back from reaching a new way of life.

Only the fighting truth can beat these Amalekite bandits. Consider that. What other approach could they use? Moses and the Israelites couldn't sweet-talk these Amalekites into leaving them alone. Imagine Moses, under a white flag of truce, approaching the Amalekite camp saying, "Listen, gentlemen, do you think you could find someone else to attack? We appreciate your special needs, but perhaps you could think of our needs as well?" That approach just wouldn't work. Moses would become their next victim. We can't sweet-talk our negative thoughts either. They don't care how we feel; these Amalekites are bad through and through. If we entertain them, we necessarily become their victims. Amalekites eat nice guys for breakfast!

The Amalekite-thoughts can't be reasoned with either. In our own lives, we sometimes do try to reason with negative thoughts. They start their negative chatter, and we counter with really good rational arguments. But they counter with even more lies. For instance, if you are suffering from guilt, you might tell the Amalekites, "I know I've done wrong, but at least God forgives me." They counter with, "Oh yeah? I wouldn't be so sure." The Amalekites might tempt you to start slinging mud at your spouse. You may reason with them, "That type of response will make things worse." They immediately reply, "You've got exactly six seconds to start slinging before she slings the mud your way. If you don't shoot first, she'll knock you so flat you won't be able to look her in the eye for a year!" If you are afraid to fly and you reason with the Amalekites by telling them, "Statistically, flying is safer than driving," they reply, "Oh yeah? Tell that to the 170 passengers who went down in New York last week. Crashes happen. Somebody dies. Why not this plane, and you?"

You can't reason with your destructive thoughts. You can't sweet-talk them into leaving you alone either. They are ruthless bandits who want nothing more than for you to beg them, promise them anything, and cry for mercy, while they laugh and cruelly abuse you. The only way to win is to enlist the fighting truth. Joshua and his army must be commissioned to do battle against these foes.

In practical terms, this means that we must use what truth we know to fight the negative thoughts that enter our minds. When a negative thought ambushes us, we must counter with a true thought, or many true thoughts, to fight against it. We don't reason or sweet-talk with that truth, because we don't allow the negative thought to answer. This is not two-way communication. This is not a dialogue, not a debate. This is a soliloquy that we speak as if our life depended on it—because it does! We state the truth convincingly in our minds, hold onto it, repeat it, and keep it fresh before us, until the negative thought is beaten back and retreats.

This technique for battling the negative thoughts is not new. It comes from a very trustworthy source, as related in the gospel of Matthew. Jesus himself, when he went into his own wilderness for forty days, was tempted by the devil. He too used the fighting truth to counter the devil's lies. He, so to speak, relied on Joshua to conquer the Amalekites. Every time the devil tempted him to do something wrong he would respond with a quotation from Scripture. When Jesus hungered, the devil told him to turn a stone into bread. He replied, "Man shall not live by bread alone, but by every word that proceeds from the mouth of God" (Matt. 4:4). Satan tempted him to throw himself off the pinnacle of the temple. Jesus replied, "It is written again, 'You shall not tempt the Lord your God'" (Matt. 4:7). Finally, the devil told him that he would receive all the wealth of the world if only Jesus would worship him. Jesus replied, "Away with you, Satan! For it is written, 'You shall worship the Lord your

God, and Him only you shall serve'" (Matt. 4:10). Jesus fought his spiritual foes using the truth often. Perhaps this is why he said, "I came not to bring peace but a sword" (Matt. 10:34).

You and I can also summon the fighting truth to protect ourselves against the nasty thoughts that often attack us. True thoughts and ideas wait to be enlisted to battle our spiritual foes. Sometimes these true ideas come from Sacred Scripture, from a self-help book we've been reading, or from daily affirmations. We can send them out to do battle with the enemy.

If you suffer from insecurity and a fear of abandonment and the negative thoughts begin to pour in, you can counter with many familiar sayings from the Scripture. You might repeat to yourself, "Yea, though I walk through the valley of the shadow of death, I will fear no evil; for you are with me." You might repeat that last sentence, or one like it, again and again: "For you are with me. For you, O God, are with me. I have nothing to fear." You might repeat the phrase from Psalm 31, "In you, O Lord, I put my trust. Let me never be ashamed." You might repeat and meditate on Jesus's comforting words to his disciples, "Lo, I am with you always, even unto the end of the age." These familiar sayings can comfort you and create an inner sensation that you are supported and not alone. You can learn that you will never be abandoned, because you will always have God with you. You will recognize that you don't need to cling, badger, control, or abuse. The negative thoughts that urge you on begin to retreat. They have lost the battle.

In another instance, if you find yourself becoming angry at someone, you might quietly repeat the phrase "Live and let live" over and over again. You might shout it out in your own mind to counter the voices that urge you to strike out and verbally attack. You might repeat the phrase "Do to others as you would have them do to you"; or "Forgive and you will be forgiven"; or maybe something completely different, such as "Let go and let God," which brings a sense of relief and helps you to get a grip on yourself before you lash out at others.

I know that, when I am flying, saying the Serenity Prayer has helped me calm down. I also have meditated on God's providential care and have repeated to myself, "God wants me on this plane. I am in the perfect place at the perfect time." That comes from a spiritual-growth course a colleague of mine teaches in Tucson. In my first opportunity to try it I was on the flight home from a set of meetings in Tucson. The weather conditions were terrible that day. We had taken off smoothly; but, while descending for a quick stop in Albuquerque, we encountered heavy turbulence, and the plane bounced 200 feet! (At least that's what the Amalekites say. It was probably more like five feet.) My heart shot into my throat; I thought I'd choke on it. Cathy was asleep beside me. I grabbed her hand and told her we were "going down!" She mumbled sleepy-eyed, "Oh, that's nice. Let me know when we reach the terminal."

Needless to say, the phrase "I am in the perfect place at the perfect time" didn't work well that day, at that altitude. And truthfully, many passengers did think something was wrong. Also, the pilot apologized over the intercom; and after we landed, he came out and apologized to each one of us. (I was glad that he chose not to do this during the flight itself.) But I have tried that little phrase on subsequent flights, accompanied by some relaxation techniques, and it has worked wonders. A combination of flying often and thinking about the thousands of flights that take place each day without incident really helped me too. Most of the time now, the Amalekite can't get a seat beside me. Joshua is there, holding a magazine, with one eye on it and one eye on the Amalekite sitting two rows up on the right.

The truth really is that powerful. In times of struggle and temptation, bring the truth to mind. Concentrate on it, use it as a sword to fight your inner adversaries and their lies. You will find that the Amalekites will begin to retreat. No false idea can withstand the truth. It will lead you, guide you, and protect you. As Jesus said, "You shall know the truth, and the truth will set you free" (John 8:32).

Raise Your Hands to Heaven

When Joshua went out to fight the Amalekites, Moses promised that he would take his rod and climb to the top of the hill in view of the battle. He would help Joshua win the battle by raising his hands toward heaven. In fact, when the battle began and Moses did raise his hands, Joshua and his Israelite army began to defeat the enemy soundly. When Moses put his hands down, they began to lose. So Moses kept his arms raised, helped at times by Aaron and Hur, until Joshua won the battle. Israel tasted its first glorious and decisive victory.

How do we raise our hands in times of spiritual battle? Try physically doing it yourself. If you can, right now, raise both hands to heaven and look up. Go ahead. Try it. What kind of body language is being used there? What is that action saying? What do you feel you are saying when you do that? For me, it feels as if I'm looking up to and calling upon a power greater than myself. It acknowledges through body language that someone up there somewhere can help me, and with arms raised, I am asking for that help. Try raising your hands and looking up again. Can you see what I'm talking about?

Moses' action represents acknowledging a power greater than self. As long as Moses keeps his hands up, the Israelites win the battle. When he drops them, the Israelites begin to lose. Isn't that the same in our spiritual lives? Sometimes, especially in spiritual temptation or turmoil, we can easily see that we can't make progress alone. We gladly raise our head and our hands to heaven, and call upon God as we understand him to deliver us from our spiritual foe. And to the degree that we turn it over to God and let him do the fighting, we are victorious. But often, especially after a string of successes over our destructive tendencies, we forget the real source of power. We lower our hands, turn our heads down, and subsequently begin to lose the battle. To continue in victory, we must raise them toward God, and ask for divine help.

Moses' raising and lowering of his arms illustrates several important spiritual lessons. For one, we will fluctuate between acknowledging a power greater than self and trying to do it on our own—we too will raise our hands, so to speak, and lower them. At times we will lose the battle to the Amalekites, or other spiritual enemies that lurk within, and at times we will celebrate glorious victory. We shouldn't be disheartened by this. We shouldn't be afraid to ask for support either. Remember: Aaron and Hur helped Moses to keep his arms up at one point. Aaron was a priest and Hur a lay leader. This suggests that we need the support of our own understanding of spiritual principles (Aaron), as well as physical and emotional support (Hur), during these tough times. Also, when Moses became really tired, he rested on a large rock. This symbolizes resting on the Rock of Ages, the blessed assurance that God can defeat our spiritual foes. We can rely on that knowledge, trust in it, and keep our hands raised toward heaven.

On our spiritual journey, that means not only relying on the fighting truth to help defeat our negative attackers, but also recognizing and calling upon a power greater than self to take command and win the battle for us. In times of fear we've got to submit our will and our lives to God and say to him, as Jesus did, in all trust and sincerity, "Father, into your hands I commend my spirit" (Luke 23:46). When tempted to hurt or control others, we can focus upward and quietly ask God to help us do what is right. He will pour new strength into us to bolster our resistance against those Amalekites. We will not lose the battle and hurt those we love. In all times of spiritual battle, if we lift up our thoughts toward God and ask for help, he will fill us with new strength, power, and resolve, and we will triumph over our spiritual enemies.

Years ago I had a dream about flying. I wasn't in a plane, nor did I have wings. I flew on my own. Practically all of us have dreamed

of flying and know how delightful it can be. In my dream, every time
I raised my hands and head upward, I would begin to fly. I felt as if
I were being lifted up and supported by an invisible power. I was
filled with comfort and peace. When I awoke, I reflected on my
dream and realized that it reminded me of an event from my every-
day life, but I couldn't figure out what. Later that day, my eldest son,
Ronnie, who was only a toddler, came to me and put both his hands
into the air in my direction, signaling me to pick him up. As I put my
hands under his arms and lifted him into the air, I was struck by the
similarity of this action to that of my dream, only in the dream I was
the child lifting my hands for someone else to raise me up. I also realized that the "someone else" who lifted me was the invisible power
that has always lifted me up. Later I reflected that this is what is
meant by becoming as a little child in order to enter the kingdom of
heaven. Perhaps what we must do is simply raise our hands, like a
child, to our heavenly Father for support. Can we have that innocence, that trust that if we raise our head and hands God will be there
to lift us up, to deliver us from turmoil, to allow us to fly toward
heaven and rest in the comfort of his tender care? We can become
as little children and raise our hands on high toward the Father who
can help us. The help is always there, even as he helped Moses and
the Israelites in the battle against the Amalekites. All we need to do
is lift our arms, like a child, towards our Father in heaven.

The Magical Rod

One other notable element supplements this story. When Moses
lifted his hands he grasped his rod firmly between them. He was
told to take his rod and lift it up. This sounds familiar. He had used
the rod many times before. If we briefly review each time he used
the rod thus far, we can recognize its important role in Israel's journey and also in our own spiritual development. It is also extraordinary to find out what ultimately happened to the rod.

Remember, the rod was made of wood. It was a simple stick.
It symbolizes the power of goodness or the good that comes

naturally to us. When we first heard of this rod, Aaron threw it down before pharaoh and it became a snake. This represented a warning in our own minds from the Divine that, if we do not move forward out of the slavery of our own egos, what little good we know will become sensual. The next time we saw the rod, the children of Israel were trapped at the Red Sea, a predicament that symbolized the apparently overwhelming impasses we meet in our spiritual lives. We feel as though we simply can't move forward. But Moses was told to lift his rod up and point it forward—we can lift up what little good we know, make it a priority, and that seeming impasse will part. We will move forward into a new life. Then we saw the children of Israel before the rock of Horeb, thirsting for water. Moses struck the rock with his rod symbolizing the way each of us must tap into the facts we know with a sincere desire to do good. Whenever we do this a great miracle takes place. The rock is struck and living truth pours forth.

Now, once again Moses is told to take up that rod. When spiritual enemies attack, the rod still has great power. Lift it up. Lift up the little good you have in your life, your desire to be of help to others and to be loving. Make it a priority, and the negative thoughts will begin to break apart and fall away. Becoming active and useful is a great way to rid yourself of these Amalekites. There really is something to the phrase "Idleness is the devil's pillow." If you raise the good you carry in your heart above self, by expressing it in acts of charity and usefulness, the negative thoughts will begin to retreat. Try it. If you are depressed, feeling guilty, becoming resentful, get busy and do something charitable. Become productive. See if the negative thoughts that have been ambushing begin to diminish. They will, even as the Amalekites began to diminish when Moses took up his rod and raised his hands to heaven.

But the last story about the rod is certainly the best. This time it is Aaron's rod. Aaron's rod, at least in the beginning, represents simple, rudimentary good. It is not the real and living love and charity we later develop in our hearts and in our deeds. It is just the basic mentality of "keep-your-head-straight,-live-and-let-live,-be-kind." But as we progress through the wilderness it doesn't remain rudimentary. When viewed metaphorically, what happens to the rod is truly astounding. Aaron puts his rod in the ground with all the Israelites' rods around his. The next day it blooms! His rod blossoms forth like a fragrant, flowering fruit tree, containing leaves for the healing of the nations! When viewed spiritually, of course it blossoms! Through our journey toward the promised land, through our struggles and our victories over our spiritual enemies, that simple goodness becomes deeper, more spiritual, more pure, more heavenly, and certainly more powerful; it blossoms to become fragrant and living. The good we cherish yearns to blossom forth into every facet of our lives. Its power and beauty are astounding.

Victory

Joshua and his army enjoyed a great victory over the Amalekites. Before this battle they had not known war. But this battle had strengthened them. Even though they may not have known how to fight; even though they may not have had many weapons; even though these Amalekites knew the landscape well, had been fighting for years, and were ruthless killers, God was on the Israelites' side. No matter how vulnerable, weak, or incompetent they had felt, if they bolstered their fight with a sincere trust that God would deliver them, with Moses on that hill, hands raised to heaven, Joshua in the trenches shouting out commands and leading the Israelites forward into battle, no enemy could defeat them. They were truly invincible.

In our spiritual growth and our internal battles, we may not know exactly how to fight the negative thoughts that enter our minds; we may not feel confident that we can beat the spiritual enemies that harass us when we are down. We may not feel strong enough to endure such a confrontation now or ever. But God is on our side. He is ready to help. If only we raise our thoughts up to heaven and request that help, we will find the strength to win any battle. If we allow the truth to fight for us, we will defeat the destructive thoughts and negative emotions that attack us, trap us, and stifle our growth. If we make doing good our highest priority, no spiritual enemy can block our path. We too, with God on our side, can become truly invincible.

Exercises

1. Identify the Amalekites in your life. What lies do they tell you, and how do they hurt you?

2. In times of inward struggle or confusion, raise your hands, that is, look up to a higher power for help. If you are alone, actually lift your head and raise your hands to heaven, and vocally ask God for help. Does this help with the struggle?

READINGS

Then the Lord said to Moses, "Go to the people and sanctify them today and tomorrow, and let them wash their clothes. And let them be ready for the third day. For on the third day the Lord will come down upon Mount Sinai in the sight of all the people.". . . . Then it came to pass on the third day, in the morning, that there were thunderings and lightnings, and a thick cloud on the mountain; and the sound of the trumpet was very loud, so that all the people who were in the camp trembled. And Moses brought all of the people out of the camp to meet with God, and they stood at the foot of the mountain. Now Mount Sinai was completely in smoke, because the Lord descended upon it in fire. . . . Then the Lord came down upon Mount Sinai, on the top of the mountain. And the Lord called Moses to the top of the mountain, and Moses went up. . . . And God spoke all these words, saying: "I am the Lord your God, who brought you out of the land of Egypt, out of the house of bondage. You shall have no other gods before me. You shall not make for yourselves any carved image. . . . You shall not take the name of the Lord your God in vain. . . . Remember the Sabbath day, to keep it holy. Six days you shall labor and do all your work, but the seventh day is the Sabbath of the Lord your God. In it you shall do no work. . . . Honor your father and your mother. . . . You shall not murder. You shall not commit adultery. You shall not steal. You shall not bear false witness against your neighbor. You shall not covet your neighbor's house . . . nor anything that is your neighbor's." Exodus 19:10-20; 20:1-17

CHAPTER SEVEN

Personal Revelations
Sinai

In the Ancient Church holy worship was held upon mountains . . .
because mountains symbolize the celestial things of love.

Arcana Coelestia 2722

At the Foot of the Mountain

The Israelites had journeyed out of the flat lands of Egypt,
through a barren wilderness, and into the hill country. Eventually
they found themselves at the foot of an awesome mountain called
Sinai. These men and women who had never seen anything quite
as immense as Sinai and the mountains that surrounded it must have
been amazed by the sight. They were told to set up camp at the foot
of this majestic mountain. They were told to prepare themselves
here, for their God would appear to them in this place. The God
who had delivered them from Egypt, who had split the waters of
the Red Sea, who had fed them bread and water in the wilderness,
who had given them victory over their enemies would actually
reveal himself to them on this mountain, as soon as they could make
themselves ready.

In our spiritual journey, you and I, like the Israelites, come
before a magnificent mountain. Most of our journey has been
through a flatland wilderness; we looked down toward the dust of
the earth, kept our nose to the grindstone of spiritual growth. As
we began to journey upward toward a more spiritual way of life,
we kept our gaze only a few feet in front of us, constantly searching for spiritual nourishment and shelter. Often we glanced

121

cautiously behind rather than optimistically ahead, reflecting on past spiritual enemies, those destructive thoughts, which so often would attack us by surprise. But now, at least for the time being, we can leave our enemies behind. Now, as we come nearer to a promised way of life, we begin to relax. Soon we begin to focus ahead and recognize the towering mountain of potential for goodness that lies ahead. We gaze up in awe at the vast potential for a happy life, for wholeness and spirituality. It can fill us with a sense of wonder and anticipation.

Mountains represented what is holy to the Israelites. We read in Isaiah 2:3, "Come, and let us go up to the mountain of the Lord, to the house of the God of Jacob; He will teach us His ways, and we shall walk in His paths." And Psalm 72:3 states, "The mountains will bring peace to the people, and the little hills, through righteousness." Mountains represent what is heavenly, what is holy in our spiritual lives as well. Climbing the mountain symbolizes elevating our comprehension so that we can receive revelation from God, so that he can teach us, even as he taught the Israelites by giving the Ten Commandments at Sinai. Israel's coming before this mountain symbolizes a positive state of spiritual enlightenment and understanding.

This is important. Life is not one continual struggle. Certainly, we find ourselves fighting destructive thoughts such as the Amalekites or other spiritual enemies. But we find ourselves at the foot of Sinai as well. Every time we have a vision of our spiritual potential, we stand at the foot of Sinai. Every time we have a breakthrough in our comprehension of God, we stand at the foot of Sinai. We don't find ourselves fighting the Amalekites or other enemies every day. Sometimes we consciously stand at the brink of a vast potential for spiritual growth. It is a time of peace and of hope, of wonder, and even excitement, because the Divine speaks to us from this mountain. Even as God gave the Ten Commandments to the Israelites, he gives us clear instructions about how to find happiness. We, too, receive revelation. It doesn't appear in the form of two stone tablets, but God does speak to us. He begins to speak through the conscience, the human rationality and perception, in the teachings of religion. We can come to see that this God we've been following through the wilderness truly is alive and real, omniscient and omnipresent.

Prepare to Meet Your God

The children of Israel were told to prepare themselves to meet their God. They should not approach the mountain until they were ready. They should wash themselves and their clothes, make themselves presentable for their God. Imagine thousands upon thousands of people cleaning themselves up, laundering their clothes, combing their hair, polishing their sandals, and making themselves beautiful for their God. It must have been something special to see!

The symbolic meaning of these actions is important for our spiritual lives. Just as the children of Israel had to prepare themselves to meet their God, we can prepare ourselves. Like the Israelites, we are warned not to go upon the mountain too soon, jumping into a new way of life without thorough preparation. God warns us to take our time, to know our limits. If we run up the mountain of holiness, into a completely new and spiritual way of life, we won't be able to stay. It would be too abrupt; our understanding of that way of life hasn't become deep and lasting; our willingness to stay in a loving or spiritual state hasn't developed. We must not act impulsively. Every step toward a spiritual life must be mindful and prudent.

It may be tempting not to take time spiritually, to rush headlong into new programs and ideas to promote spiritual life without much forethought or preparation. Some people have tried one religion after another, or one self-help philosophy after another, feeling dizzily motivated by the new ideas, making some progress; and then, a short time later, suddenly feeling deflated, disappointed, perhaps even betrayed. Those programs may have been very worthwhile, but to embrace them as though they were the only true messiah that could heal their terminal disease is asking for disappointment. When they found out that these programs weren't the messiah, only helpful teachers, they reacted negatively, angrily. But where does the real problem lie? It lies within the expectation. God has a lesson for everyone: look before you leap. Don't embrace a new philosophy or a new way of life, even if it seems right for you, until you are prepared to offer your best self and give it your best effort. Know your limits. Don't climb every mountain in search of God. Instead, prepare yourself, make yourself ready at the foot of the hill; and, if you are truly ready, God will make himself known to you.

Like the children of Israel, individuals must cleanse themselves and make themselves ready to receive new revelation from the Divine. How do people cleanse themselves? In biblical terms it's simple: they repent. In today's terms, it's just as simple: they clean up their act. In the words of Isaiah 1:16-18, both metaphors are used: "Wash yourselves, make yourselves clean; put away the evils of your doings from before my eyes. Cease to do evil, learn to do well; seek justice, reprove the oppressor; defend the fatherless, plead for the widow. Come now, let us reason together, says the Lord, though your sins be as scarlet, they shall be as white as snow." To experience a vision of the Divine and receive insight and revelation from the Divine, individuals must put their lives into order. If they don't prepare a way for God to come to them, God cannot come. In other words, God's ability to make himself known to individuals is directly proportionate to their ability to make themselves ready to receive God. If their outward lives are contrary to his love, forgiveness, and healing, they can't receive his gifts.

How often do human beings ask God for help without actively making any changes to allow God to help them? It happens a lot. How many people who suffer from alcoholism have asked God for help between gulps from the bottle but somehow never take the action to put the bottle down? How many people have been stuck in a rut in their relationship and have said, "God, help me!" but have not opened their minds to see the other person's point of view? How many people have cried desperately for a more meaningful relationship with God, but have allowed their lives to consist of nothing more than work, sleep, and television? They wonder, between episodes of *General Hospital* and *All My Children,* why their lives are so lonely and devoid of spirituality. God is unable to help these people until they begin to help themselves, until they order their lives in such a way that God can manifest himself to them and help them. If they need help with an addiction or compulsion, they need to seek help, find a center for help or a twelve-step meeting. If they want a more loving, giving relationship, they must make the first move toward becoming more loving and giving. If they want spirituality, they've got to make room for spirituality. God speaks in a still, small voice. They won't hear it over the blaring television.

Each of us has the potential to know, to understand, and to feel the divine presence. If we have escaped the slavery of our destructive inclinations and have begun a search for a better way of life, God will begin to reveal himself to us. But we must make ourselves ready, make ourselves clean, lose those character defects, abstain from so much sensual input, till we can hear God's call and feel his gentle touch. We must stop the continual partying or the incessant arguing or the workaholism, the fear, the control, the manipulation; we must repair and make ready the parts of our lives that prevent us from being with our God. We must turn off the television or the stereo, get quiet, and wait for our God. We must wait and listen at the foot of that mountain.

God Comes in the Clouds

The Israelites made themselves ready within three days and God did not disappoint them. He appeared right on time. A trumpet sounded from out of nowhere in the morning, and it seemed to become louder and louder. Moses led the people, now sanctified and prepared, to the foot of the mountain, where they witnessed an awesome sight. Thick smoke descended onto the mountain, lightening flashed, thunder boomed, the mountain quivered and shook. God descended in a flame. Moses spoke to God, and God answered him by voice! The people trembled with fear, but Moses instructed them to hold their ground. They were filled with a holy fear and wonder.

Spiritually, this extraordinary scene symbolized God's emerging presence in our conscious lives. We can begin to sense some real conscious contact with God. The familiar fire of his love burns before us. His voice speaks in the form of our conscience. The lightning flashes: insights are revealed. Thunder shakes the mountain: we sense the power of this creative force called God. We can tremble with a holy fear as we recognize that we are not alone, that we have never been alone, and never will be. God is real. It's a scary realization! In fact, the Israelites came to Moses and said, "*You* speak for us, Moses. We don't want to talk to God. We're afraid of all this!" But Moses told them to hold fast and endure this magnificent scene.

Have you seen God on the mountain? If you've been trying to lead a spiritual life, you probably have. It doesn't happen every day. Just as we don't fight the Amalekites every day, neither do these tremendous visions of God swoop down every day. But they do come. They come in the form of our conscience, the tender voice of the Divine directing us so quietly. In times of inner peace, when we've prepared ourselves to hear the voice of the Divine, we are often given new insights into life. Sometimes they illuminate our minds like lightening. Sometimes a new outlook or a fresh answer to an old problem can shake our minds like thunder. We sense the Divine's presence within those flashes of enlightenment, within the inner voices of conscience. Sometimes God's open communication with us can become downright eerie. A great number of people have reported the following experience: they have picked up the Bible and asked God a question, and opened the Bible to a random page for the answer. Those who have done this have told me that God speaks in a remarkable way through the verses they selected

at random. Sometimes it can even be frightening when God openly speaks in his written revelation, whatever form that may take.

The revelation I often turn to, like many, is the Bible. I opened
the Bible on an occasion when I was truly in need of an answer.
This particular time God gave me his answer, right between the
eyes. I was plagued by serious doubts about my vocation. At one
time I had felt called to the ministry, summoned to do God's work.
In fact, I had even felt that I'd been called to do his work in some
major way. For me, this calling was important to remember and
honor. But after working as a minister for a couple of years, I realized that I would never make any money doing God's work and
that I might be better off securing a job in advertising or public relations, where I could make two or three times more money. After all,
most of what I was doing was advertising and public relations for
the church anyway. Why not do it for someone else and cash in?
So, ignoring my call and pursuing that glittering god called
Mammon seemed more and more appealing. As I lost myself in fantasies about dropping out of the ministry to make the big bucks, I
completely lost sight of the call. Although I felt a little guilty, I was
ready to make the move. I decided to assuage my guilt by asking
God one more time what I should do. Perhaps if I got out the Bible,
closed my eyes, opened the book anywhere and randomly pointed
my finger to one or two verses, God would lead me to the final
answer. (I am sure, in retrospect, that, at least subconsciously, I
didn't expect a clear answer that would justify my decision—it
would prove that God didn't care, or maybe even that he didn't
really exist, and that I could leave my job to go for the gold!)

I closed my eyes, opened the book, put my finger on a page,
opened my eyes and read Mark 8:36: "For what will it profit a man
if he gains the whole world, and loses his own soul?" Boom! That's
the only way to describe the effect of those words. Boom! They
burst my whole illusionary bubble. Suddenly I realized that I faced
a blatant temptation to walk away from God. I realized that I really
would lose my soul, my inner life and spark, and real happiness and

joy, if I quit the ministry. I realized that I had, indeed, been called. It was a true call, from deep within, that constituted my very character as a human being. I couldn't turn my back on that. I would be walking away from myself and my true purpose in life. That night God spoke directly to my heart. I have not doubted my calling since, and—for the most part—I love my job. Think of all the passages I could have turned to, but that one verse was where God led me. Is it a coincidence? For me it was no coincidence. That verse was, in that moment, God's voice, thundering into my consciousness.

God reveals himself on that mountain in a lot of different ways to a lot of different people. Most people don't talk directly with God—or if they do, they're not telling us about it. But the Divine does come to us and speak with us in a variety of ways: in our conscience, in flashes of enlightenment; in new insights; in reflective thoughts; in nature; in the voices of loved ones; in all the revelations and the religions of the world. Sometimes the divine voice can be so vivid and open that it is hard to doubt. But enough room is left for doubt. Even when God appeared to the Israelites, it was on a stormy day within the smoke of the fire and the clouds. Those who wanted to doubt could always claim it was "smoke and mirrors." "God didn't really appear on the mountain," they might say. "It was just a combination of a good thunder storm, a forest fire, and a couple of trumpeters hiding behind the bushes." God always leaves some room for doubt, but clearly, miracles can occur for those who believe in God and listen for him. In truth, when we make ourselves ready, God can make himself known to us in the clouds of our own minds, speak to us within our thoughts, and give us the direction we need to conduct a happy and productive life.

The Giving of the Law

What was so significant about God's giving Moses the Ten Commandments? The Israelites knew these commandments. Egypt had the same rules; so did every developed nation of the world. Why were they delivered in such a miraculous way to

Israel? So that the Israelites would see that these laws were not just civil laws, but divine laws. These were not simply the laws of men but the laws of God.

At some point in spiritual development, we can begin to recognize that the laws of religion such as the Ten Commandments, or the Golden Rule, or laws about loving others are not simply rules placed on society for the sole purpose of keeping order; these laws are divine. They don't just help people maintain order in this world; they lead to spirituality. They lead to heaven and a heavenly way of life. We can come to the recognition that these rules lead to happiness, fulfilled dreams, to real life!

That is why when God first began to give the Ten Commandments he said, "I am the Lord your God, who brought you out of the land of Egypt, out of the house of bondage" (Exodus 20:2). He identified himself to the children of Israel as the God who had helped them escape their bondage. Spiritually, we can realize that this God whom we have followed cares deeply for us. He gives us these rules of life to promote our happiness. In all of our spiritual struggles to date, God has always been there to help. Now, in an enlightened state, we can appreciate what he has done, and we come to a solid recognition that God is a good God, and what he teaches us is good, and leads to good. This is what is represented when God gives the Law at Sinai.

The Golden Calf

The children of Israel were not completely loyal to Moses and God at this time. In fact, when Moses went to the mountain to receive the Ten Commandments, they constructed a golden calf and worshiped that calf, calling it their god. Spiritually, this symbolizes the confused state we remain in, even in our time of new insight and revelation. Like Israel, we do not yet dwell in the promised land of a new way of life. We are just beginning to experience victory over some of our shortcomings. We are just beginning to experience conscious contact with God. But we don't completely understand who

God is and aren't completely willing to worship him. Part of us would still like to claim credit for the changes we've made and give credit to some secular explanation for our progress. We are tempted, like Israel, to worship our own graven images.

Of all people, Moses' brother Aaron urges the Israelites to make the graven image. When it is finished, he proclaims to the people, "This is your god, O Israel, that brought you out of the land of Egypt!" (Exodus 32:4). Aaron, you may recall, represents human understanding of the truth. In this state of progress and some spiritual illumination, we can so easily lose sight of who really saved us from the bondage of our own destructive tendencies. It's so easy to conclude that we have led ourselves out of Egypt, so easy to form some god, like a new program, psychology, or way of thought we claim has saved us.

Cattle were common idols of worship in ancient times, especially among the Egyptians. Cattle were symbols of worldly abundance, blessing, fertility. The making of the golden calf symbolizes how we form the opinion that some worldly image of our own making has been leading us, that our success has sprung from human ingenuity, been fashioned by human hands, and is not the product of the Divine working in and through us.

Upon seeing such a perversion, Moses broke the tablets (commandments). His action symbolizes how divine laws of order can be obliterated when individuals believe they are the source of their own power and destiny. Suddenly real insights vanish into bits of dust and powder. Moses' grinding up the calf, putting it in the water, and making the Israelites drink from it symbolize the bitter recognition that man-made gods are useless, lifeless, and void of spirituality.

For example, many who have beaten the problem of addiction or compulsion through a program of recovery have nearly or actually relapsed because they lost sight of who really helped them and brought them to their new state of well-being. In a typical scenario, a woman accepts God's help, and makes great strides; but after a while, she forgets about a higher power and thinks, "Wow, I really have done wonders with myself, haven't I?" Or she might say, "My ability to resist temptation is unbelievable. My sheer willpower has saved me. It's remarkable!" That belief in self, or belief in her willpower, is that woman's golden calf. Soon though, she begins to lose sight of the program for recovery. Because she claims power for herself, the truths she used to know about relying on a higher power, turning it over to God, keeping humble, disappear. They are obliterated, like the first set of commandments were obliterated. In a time of desperation, preferably before she goes back to drinking or using, she is slapped back to her senses by some incident, or some voice of conscience—some realization symbolized by Moses—and is forced to accept the bitter truth, that her new life without chemical dependency had nothing to do with her own power at all. She senses she has been a fool to think it had. It is a bitter truth to swallow, but she swallows it and moves on.

The beauty of leading the spiritual life is that *we can move on.* Moses climbed back up that mountain, after the children of Israel repented of their ways and received the commandments again. God always waits for us to return to him. He stands forever at the top of that mountain waiting for our return, waiting for us to renew our covenant with him and take up his calling once again.

The Ark of the Covenant

When Moses was on Mt. Sinai, God not only gave him the Ten Commandments but also instructed him to build an ark in which to house them and a tabernacle in which to house the ark. A whole book could be written on the Ark of the Covenant and the tabernacle. Numerous details explained how it should be built, what it should be used for, what role it should play in the Israelites' life. In general terms, the ark was a beautiful wooden chest, overlaid with gold, with two golden cherubim (angels) on top whose wings met in the center. In it rested the two tablets containing the Ten Commandments. This was the most special and holy object in the Israelites' world. The ark was kept in the tabernacle, which was an elaborate tent-like structure that could be dismantled and moved along with the Israelites for the remainder of their journey to and into the promised land. The tabernacle was a portable temple. It became the center and focal point of their reality because it was God's dwelling place with Israel. Though an elaborate tent, it became his holy temple, to accompany them wherever they went.

Spiritually, the building of the ark and the tabernacle symbolizes the building of a place for God's laws, and thus God himself, to dwell within us. The divine law becomes inscribed in our hearts. We, like the Israelites, can take him with us wherever we go. Spirituality isn't reserved for Sunday mornings, or for those brief occasions when we are alone and feeling reflective. We can reach a point in our spiritual lives when, in some small way, God is always with us. Of course, as we struggle through life, we will lose sight of him from time to time, but he will always be with us in a new way. That is the promise of rebirth and spiritual regeneration. God becomes the center of our lives, an active force, someone we can always turn to for comfort and advice.

My Visit to the Mountain

I know that I actually need to get away at times and go into the mountains or woods. Let me tell you about the first time I took time out to find God. It was another life-changing experience for me, an affirmation of God's presence in my life. One time I had been experiencing some grave challenges on the work front. A few prominent members of my small church decided to leave for their own personal reasons, a decision that had a deeply negative effect on the rest of the congregation. Their departure also really hurt me and caused me to wonder whether the church might be in trouble. The pressure of trying to put the church back together and lead it toward growth became very great. In the spring, I finally decided that I needed to get into the north woods of Wisconsin (a place our family would often go for summer vacations) to get a little break and to see if God had any answers for me. Like a soldier, I wanted to know my new orders. So, I secured a few days of early vacation and headed off with my dog on a seven-hour trip to the north woods. I would stay there (at the foot of the mountain) for a number of days hoping to receive a message.

God didn't immediately appear before me and give me new directions, but it didn't take long to *sense* his message. Taking a few walks in the woods, under the budding trees stirred by the whispering wind, beside the lapping lake waters, and within range of the occasional call of the loon, I sensed the truth of my situation. I began to feel that actually all was well in God's world, and that I just needed to accept this. After a few days I could really feel this deeply, but still intellectually wanted some concrete answers.

The last day before packing up to go home, I stepped outside for a bike-ride to a local town five miles away. As I walked out and looked into the sky, I stopped and asked God, "Are you going to give me my orders?" I rode off down a beaten path toward town.

After I had traveled four of the five miles to town, my problems started to happen. First, I noticed the front wheel of my bicycle was off-center with the handle bars. Seconds later I found out why, as the handle bars came off in my hands, and I fell off my bike crashing gently into a grass embankment. I couldn't believe it. Was this God's answer? Nothing seemed to work anymore. Here I was four miles from my cabin, a mile from town, with a broken bike on the ground and handle bars in my hands. Everything seemed to be literally falling apart. At that point I began to panic. A voice came into my head (probably an Amalekite), strongly warning me, "It's gonna get dark soon. You better pick that bike up and walk all the way home. Walk home right now!"

Focusing on my predicament, I attempted to place the handle bars back into their slot and found that I could hold them in the right place with one hand and steer with the other. That way I could keep riding, but it would be a slow and dangerous trip. As I mounted my bike and looked behind me toward the long trip home, and ahead toward the town only a mile away, another more gentle voice spoke within, "Let go. Ride into town. It will be okay." So I decided to go forward; with one hand holding the bike together, the other steering the way, I peddled toward town.

When I arrived in town, I stopped at the only shop on the main street that was open. It was a Native-American jewelry and crafts shop. Upon entering the shop to ask the woman behind the counter for a wrench, I noticed her mild look of concern. I realized that being in a cabin with no running water for several days had changed my appearance. I must have looked as if I had been living in the woods; and when I approached her with scruffy beard, bed-head, dirty clothes and all, and asked her, "Can you do me a favor?" she looked even more concerned. But she did try to help. I asked if she had a wrench, because my bike had fallen apart. She said that all she had was a screwdriver. I borrowed it for about a minute, quickly realizing that not only would using a screwdriver on something that needed a wrench be pointless, but the type of wrench I needed was something I had never seen before. It was hopeless. I gave the screwdriver back to the woman and bought something for my family with my credit card to restore her faith in me and the capitalist system, and headed out the door.

Instead of beginning the long journey home, I decided to travel a little further. Again, something inside told me to go a little further out of town, and not to turn back. "Why not?" I said, and headed off in the opposite direction of home. I traveled through a quaint little park and over a bridge, and up a hill, and decided to ride around one more turn before turning back. As I took the corner, I approached a small building with two men sitting right outside the door. As I peddled closer, I noticed—and this is the honest truth— that the building was a bicycle shop. The two men were sitting outside fixing bikes! I rode up and asked them if I could borrow a special wrench to fix my handle bars. The one man held the very wrench in his hand! "Sure," he said, "No problem. But don't tighten it too hard because it will break." He smiled. I half-expected him to say,

"So, Grant, do you understand yet?" But he didn't. Amazed and dazed, I thanked them both and turned to leave for home.

That would be a great end to the story, but it goes on. Just before reaching my cabin I wondered out loud about the fact that God had shown me quite a lot those four days, but I still had never received any real orders. As I turned the last bend on the road leading to the cabin, I spotted a familiar little summer shelter built by a couple who lived next door. I could see from a sign above this tiny screened cabin that they had named the place "Tranquility." I knew that with a name like that, I had to check this place out. I set my bicycle down and walked the small path over to the door of the little cabin. Another sign appeared on the entrance door. It read, "All are welcome. But please leave everything as you found it. We love this place." That made me smile. It was easy to see that everything was built with such great care. As I entered the one room cabin, I noticed a little table in the center with two chairs, a copy of the Bible laying on the table, and a few other books underneath it. The place was well named. It felt tranquil. "Well, I guess I won't get my orders, but this is beautiful," I thought to myself. Then, looking up to the top of the wall, where it joined the ceiling, I noticed that there was an inscription etched in wood. It ran across the top of the four walls of the cabin, so that in order to read it I had to turn and face each wall as I read. It was taken from Micah 6:8: "He has shown you, O man, what is good, and what does the Lord require of you, but to act justly, and to love mercy, and to walk humbly with your God." I smiled and breathed deeply, knowing that it was time to travel home. I had received my orders.

Exercises

1. Make time to relax daily. If you are not used to relaxing, begin by scheduling ten minutes a day to sit quietly by yourself with no activities around to distract you. Force yourself to do this each day for at least one week. After that week, see how this time has begun to make a difference in your life.

2. When you say your prayers, make sure you leave at least the same amount of time to simply listen. What is God trying to tell you? What is his will for you?

So Moses sent them to spy out the land of Canaan. . . . And they returned from spying out the land after forty days. . . . Then they told him, and said, "We went to the land where you sent us. It truly flows with milk and honey, and this is its fruit. Nevertheless the people who dwell in the land are strong; more-over we saw the descendants of Anak there. . . . Then Caleb quieted the people before Moses, and said, "Let us go up at once and take possession, for we are well able to overcome it." But the men who had gone up with him said, "We are not able to go up against the people, for they are stronger than we." And they gave the children of Israel a bad report of the land which they had spied out, saying, "The land through which we have gone as spies is a land that devours its inhabitants, and all the people whom we saw in it are men of great stature. There we saw the giants . . . and we were like grasshoppers in our own sight, and so we were in their sight."   Numbers 13:17-33

And all the children of Israel murmured against Moses and Aaron, and . . . said to them, "If only we had died in the land of Egypt! Or if only we had died in the wilderness! Why has the Lord brought us to this land to fall by the sword, that our wives and children should become victims? Would it not be better for us to return to Egypt?" So they said to one another, "Let us select a leader and return to Egypt.". . . And the Lord said to Moses. . . "Truly, as I live, . . . they certainly shall not see the land of which I swore to their fathers, nor shall any of those who rejected me see it. . . . You shall by no means enter the land which I swore I would make you dwell in. But your little ones, whom you said would be victims, I will bring in, and they shall know the land which you have despised."   Numbers 14 ff.

CHAPTER EIGHT

Overcoming Fear

Giants in the Land

The old person must die before the new one can be conceived.

Arcana Coelestia 18

Israel's Predicament, Decisions, and Repercussions

Moses led the children of Israel to the border of the promised land. Only the river Jordan separated them from their final destination. There they sat, on the other side of the Jordan, poised to enter and claim this land. They sent spies in to view the territory and report on exactly what the land was like and how strong any obstructing enemy might be. Twelve spies, one from each tribe, were selected for this reconnaissance mission, one of which was Joshua, commander of Israel's army and future successor to Moses.

Imagine those men, who had traveled hundreds of miles over rocks and dust in the wilderness, crossing over into this beautiful, plush, green land, with forests and trees, ripe fields and meadows, brooks and springs, fruits and vegetation everywhere to be picked and eaten. Remember that they had lived on bread, water, and occasional quail for a long time. Though the vegetation of the land improved around them as they approached Canaan, this new land beyond the Jordan must have inspired wonder. This land flowed with milk and honey, even as God had promised.

But they also spotted many enemies who would have to be uprooted. The Amalekites, the Hittites, the Jebusites, the Amorites, the Canaanites, and still others blocked Israel's inheritance. They also recognized the children of Anak, who were said to be giants. This sight filled the majority of the spies with fear. Nevertheless, they spent a good forty days thoroughly exploring the land before they returned to Moses and the Israelites.

When the spies returned, they brought with them delicious mementos of their visit. They brought back a huge cluster of grapes, pomegranates, and figs. They told the people that, yes, the land flowed with milk and honey, but that large, well-fortified cities, many enemies, and even giants stood in their way, and would be hard to defeat. Joshua and Caleb, two of the spies, said, "Let us go up at once and take possession, for we are well able to overcome it. . . . The land we passed through to spy out is an exceedingly good land. If the Lord delights in us, then He will bring us into this land and give it to us, 'a land which flows with milk and honey'" (Numbers 13:30; 14:7-8). They knew that their God was with them; and with God on their side, they couldn't lose. But the other spies, countering Joshua and Caleb, changed their story into a negative report about the land and exaggerated the power of the enemy. They said, "The land through which we have gone as spies is a land that devours its inhabitants, and all the people whom we saw in it are men of great stature. . . . We were like grasshoppers in our own sight, and so we were in their sight" (Numbers 13:32-33).

You can just imagine how the children of Israel reacted to the negative report. They began to cry out the familiar refrain, "Let us go back to Egypt!" They cried out, "If only we had died in Egypt!" Some said, "If only we had died in the wilderness! Why has the Lord brought us to this land to fall by the sword, that our wives and our children should become victims?" (Numbers 14:2-3) They felt they had become victims of God's design. They chose a leader and made plans to return to Egypt.

Suddenly the glory of God appeared over the tabernacle, and God spoke with Moses and the people. He told them that, indeed, they would not enter the promised land after all. Their attitude, their mistrust, their selfishness, their insolence, and stiff-necked view of life were enough to stop them from entering that land. This old nation of doubters and complainers would die in the wilderness. Only their children, a new generation, born, raised, and fed out of the hand of God in the wilderness, would inherit the land. But this old generation would spend the rest of their days in the wilderness!

When the children of Israel heard this, they decided to ignore God's words. Their decision proves how defiant these people really were. As soon as God said that they *couldn't* go into the promised land, they decided they *would* go into the promised land. They decided to forget about going back to Egypt, forget what God had said. They'd go ahead after all and claim this promised land without God. No sooner had God forbidden them to take the land than they gathered their possessions and headed off without God to do just that. And as soon as they headed off, the Amalekites and Canaanites attacked them and soundly beat them back into the wilderness. Without God, they didn't stand a chance against their enemies. Sadly enough, they did spend the rest of their lives, forty more years, in the wilderness. They died there, along with Moses. A new generation, led by Joshua and Caleb, the two young men who had believed in God and the dream, would enter the land forty years later.

Our Spiritual Predicament

On the road to spiritual recovery, we will find ourselves gazing into the potential for a new way of life. It stretches out in front of us, vast, green, and plush. We are ready for a new way. We want so much to enter into a paradise of happiness, fulfilled dreams, peace, and serenity, and to enjoy the abundance of the fruits of our own labor. But enemies loom up in front of us, spiritual enemies, who seem to block our entrance. We may not see that we can move ahead. We can feel betrayed by God, as if he led us out of our old life only to die trying to reach a new one. In fact, we can feel that we've become victims of a bad divine joke. Like the Israelites, we get angry and wonder what we should do. Like the Israelites, we end up making some bad choices, and learn some hard lessons. Ultimately, we realize we must change our outlook radically, before we can enter a new way of life.

Like the Israelites, we can encounter a time in our spiritual development when we settle at the brink of a new way of life, poised to enter it. We've known the struggle in the wilderness of life. We've known hunger and thirst and have also appreciated the sustenance God has provided in our search. But now a new and bright future appears on the horizon, a future replete with hope. We begin to see what treasures life can hold if we follow our God and seek the right path. The spies sent into the land symbolize reflection upon and contemplation of the possibilities of this new, wholesome, spiritual life. It is not yet ours, even as the land of Canaan was not yet the Israelites'. But we see that it is real and, just as God had promised, a beautiful place, flowing with milk and honey.

For example, on the road of spiritual progress, sometimes traveling through a wilderness of loneliness and empty relationships, we can come upon the hope for a more meaningful and a more loving connection with those close to us. We might try out a new approach toward our associates at work, for instance, one that brings out the good qualities within them and allows them to appreciate our own. We might recognize that with a little patience and understanding, we could cultivate some very good and close friends. Our daily associations could become more meaningful, full of real care and genuine human interaction, rather than remaining the typical polite, empty conversations that they've been for the past couple of years. The potential for friendship is seen as unlimited.

On the road to spiritual progress, we can come to recognize the paradise lost, or perhaps found for the first time, in our marriage. Having survived a lot of pain and searching in marriage, hoping that love wasn't just a pipe dream, but something real to enjoy and share, we've carried on. One day, a new hope emerges; we find that the potential for friendship and mutual support, the growth we've dreamed about, can become a reality in our marriage. We notice some real fruits ripening. As the spies brought back a good bunch of grapes, we can allow our thoughts to bear fruit, to provide something more tangible than dreams. We taste their reality, though only a bit. We recognize that a beautiful friendship with our partner lies on the horizon, that tenderness and love can be ours. We envision a future together full of deep care, tenderness, and growth!

Perhaps we've searched for a promised land free from compulsion or negative thought patterns. We come to the hope and realization that we can live without the fears, the compulsions, the desire for control, the anger, the depression. We see that we can live a good life that brings nothing but milk and honey, real joy and delight. We can know peace, joy, and serenity for the first time in our lives. Whereas before we doubted these things even existed, now we believe they are real. They may not be ours to keep, but we know that they can be. That type of reflection is symbolized by the spies entering Canaan and seeing what a beautiful land it truly is, a paradise flowing with milk and honey, even as God had promised.

But milk and honey, fruit, grass, and trees are not the only features of this land. The spies see well-fortified enemy cities. This is not yet the Israelites' land. It must be fought for. Spiritually, we recognize that this new way of life isn't ours yet. Many obstacles block our ability to experience the goodness, the serenity, and the peace of mind associated with the promised land. Spiritual enemies—our destructive tendencies, character defects, and evil inclinations—stand in our way. We must uproot and kick them out of our conscious lives to become truly spiritual. We recognize that the search might be over, but the real battles have just begun.

Notice the names of these enemies in the land: the Amalekites, Hittites, Hivites, Jebusites, Perizzites. They sound like bugs, don't they? In a way they spiritually correspond to bugs, spiritual bugs, malignant enemies in our minds and our lives. They represent the anger, lust, greed, jealousy, contempt, pride, laziness, and other character defects that can torment us and ultimately block us from a happy and spiritually healthy life. In many ways, these people really did practice evil and would have contaminated the Israelites if not destroyed. Some practiced human sacrifice, passing their children through the fire, and immoral religious rituals. According to the biblical story, God told the Israelites to wipe them out because they would hurt the Israelites and pervert their religious way of life. We too must follow God's directions and annihilate these negative traits that block our spiritual progress.

Spiritually, then, we face a predicament. Looking into the future, we see the truly beautiful life we can have, but we also see the tremendous changes we will have to make. We are not sure we can make those changes, or whether we even want to. An argument begins to ensue in our minds. We go through temptation. On one side, represented by Joshua and Caleb, we see that there is great potential for us in the future, and part of us is ready to move ahead and fight whatever spiritual enemy it may be necessary to fight. But the vast majority of thoughts within us are unwilling to make those kinds of changes and fight those battles.

Joshua represents the fighting truth. It says to us, " 'Seek first the kingdom of God and his righteousness, and all these things will be added unto you.' Don't be afraid. If you believe in God and rely on his divine power, no spiritual enemy can stand before you. You will be victorious! But don't doubt!" The other thoughts counter the encouragement from Joshua and Caleb. These negative thoughts soon turn into lies and exaggerations. We think to ourselves, "My spiritual enemies are too many and too great. I'll never be able to beat them. Not only are they strongly ingrained, but they are all huge, giant problems!" We can fear our shortcomings so much that they loom up above us in our imaginations like terrible monsters and make us feel no bigger than grasshoppers in their presence.

In the literal story, the majority of the spies gave a bad report of the land. After saying that the land did, indeed, flow with milk and honey, they altered their report to say, "The land through which we have gone as spies is a land that devours its inhabitants" (Numbers 13:32). The doubts within tell us that we really didn't want to go there anyway. That land or that way of life isn't any fun. In fact, it devours its inhabitants. If we really lived like that, we'd be hurt. It would be too difficult. It would tear us apart inside, and there would be nothing left: we would be devoured!

Perhaps you can relate to these times of doubt and temptation. A person has finally glimpsed what it would be like to let go of controlling others. Part of this person is ready to let go and let God take that impulse away and wipe it out forever. But another part of this person is afraid to let go. Inner doubts murmur that this problem is too big. They say that this problem will never be conquered and that there is no use even trying. Besides, a life without control will only lead to chaos, the doubts say. It is a lifestyle that "devours its inhabitants."

Or maybe a person wants to finally break free from addiction, and part of this person has clearly observed that with help from a higher power it can be done. But doubts arise, suggesting that life would be unmanageable without one's drug of choice. It is a battle that cannot be won and should not be fought, they say. A life without that much-needed euphoria would be barren, empty, not fun at all. Whatever the situation may be, we know what our spiritual foes look like, and we can often hear those doubts exaggerate their report, telling us that all is hopeless, our enemies are too great, and that we don't want to live a new life anyway.

The Critical Mistake

What was the essential sin of the Israelites? What was their critical mistake? It was their mistrust in God. They cut him off. Look at the miracles they had witnessed in the past: how God had rescued them out of the hand of the powerful Egyptians; how he had fed the Israelites miraculously in the wilderness; how he had helped them overcome the Amalekites; how he had recently appeared to them on Sinai in a flame of fire, with smoke, thunder, lightning, and

tremors! And all they had to say for their God at this point of cru-
cial decision was that God had brought them out there to make
them victims! "We're victims!" they said.

Can we relate to that attitude? How quickly we forget how far
we've come. We can forget all the wonderful miracles that have happened to us, and the changes that have taken place in our lives. We
forget who has been leading us! We forget that God has always been
there for us. He has fed us, provided the sustenance we needed in
the wilderness, and helped us to emerge victorious over some of our
greatest spiritual enemies. We no longer live in that house of
bondage we once occupied. God has always been our champion! But
we can forget all this in times of doubt. Sometimes we absolutely
snub our God, by refusing to believe that he can help us, that there
is any power greater than ourselves. This is a real temptation.

After blaming God, the Israelites cry out, "If only we were back
in Egypt, this never would have happened." We too, once again,
think to ourselves, "If only I hadn't begun this route, everything
would be okay." Perhaps one of these refrains may ring a bell: if
only I hadn't tried to be such a nice guy, people wouldn't be taking
advantage of me. If only I had never stopped manipulating, then
I'd still have control of my daughter! If only I had continued to rip
off the company, then I wouldn't have these financial problems! If
only I hadn't followed God, then I'd be happy! That's basically
what we're saying. It's a lie, but it certainly sounds reasonable in
times of spiritual trial. Like the Israelites, we feel like victims of
God. He has dragged us out into the middle of nowhere and now
we're going to die! We long for the fantasy land of the past that
never existed. We don't realize that we are no longer in bondage.
We blame God and blame others for our unhappiness. This is the
essence of the "victim mentality."

Immediately after the Israelites' decision to abandon their mission, something incredible happened. God appeared in a cloud at
the tabernacle of meeting and said, "You will not enter the land.
You will die in the wilderness!" (Numbers 14:26-35). Imagine what

an insufferable blow that must have been to the Israelites and the irony of their situation. They had been promised a new land, but now they were going to die in the wilderness, just as they had feared. God told them that they would not enter the land because of their murmuring and discontent. He said that after their death, in forty years' time, their children would inherit the land, because their children were pure and innocent, and would follow God without doubt, denial or disobedience.

This ironic twist corresponds in our own spiritual life and development. There are two points here: first, the Israelites would remain and die in the wilderness; second, a new generation would be raised up to take the land in their stead. This symbolizes the complete change that we must make. Even as he appeared to the Israelites, God speaks to us in a powerful vision, that is, in a powerful realization. That realization is that our old self must die and a new self be born. We, as we are, cannot enter a new way of life. We must completely let go; we must completely change. Even as the cells of our body change, our spirits must change. We must be regenerated, reborn with a new attitude. Christ said to Nicodemus, "Marvel not that I say unto you, you must be born again" (John 3:7). We can't take the same old attitude with us into a new way of life. We can't take the fears with us, the mistrust, complaints, the selfish "me-first" attitude. A new generation of thoughts and feelings must be generated in order for a new way of life to begin. There comes a time when we are struck with the realization, "If I want to change my life, I've got to give it up. I've got to do it a whole new way. I've got to change completely. Part of me has got to die away, so that a new part can be born."

The Birth of a New Generation

When the children of Israel realized that God was not going to lead them into the promised land as they were, they decided to go into the promised land on their own. We try the same thing in our spiritual lives. Sometimes we reject God's call to change and decide we can do it on our own. We say to ourselves, "I don't have to change. I can do it without changing!" We try to have our cake and eat it too. We want a happy life, full of milk and honey and everything nice, but we refuse to change in order to receive it. We think we can ignore God's call for change and walk right into a new life without sacrificing a thing. Like the Israelites, we march off to capture the promised land, leaving God behind, but take all our old problems with us on the way. And the result is that our spiritual enemies beat us back badly. Like the Amalekites, they swoop down from the mountains and attack and beat us back into a wilderness of confusion and bewilderment. We can't do it without God and without changing our attitudes completely.

In this scenario we can say to ourselves, "I don't want to control anymore, so I'll only control people when I really need to." Or we might say to ourselves, "I'm only going to be anxious and afraid when those fears are really legitimate." It doesn't work. The desire for control doesn't go away. In fact, it gets worse, because now we're trying to control our desire to control. The fears don't leave either. They become more acute, because we've stimulated them by giving them credence. Like the Amalekites, they've been angered and provoked to attack. We are beaten back into our old ways.

A man suffering from alcoholism, for example, may hear the inner sentence of his conscience as he hits bottom, that his life will continue to be unmanageable unless he completely lets it go, turns his life over to a higher power, and begins a new way. And he begins. But like the Israelites, he can decide that going all the way is too tall an order. He decides that he can do it his way, without God or a higher power. In fact, he believes that he doesn't really have to change completely. He can continue to drink occasionally and still enter a new and more manageable way of life.

This is exactly what I tried to do when I first began to tackle my addiction to alcohol. (Most alcoholics try to do just that several times until they learn they can't do it alone and seek help in Alcoholics Anonymous.) I kept a notebook of my drinking episodes.

On a calendar I marked the days I stayed sober. I'd stay sober one, two, three days. Then I'd look at the calendar and congratulate myself, and then get drunk that night to celebrate. That pattern lasted for about four months until the whole scheme broke down, and I began to drink every night again. Two years later, after many a bloody battle with the Amalekites, I finally realized I must let go absolutely and go to Alcoholics Anonymous. I had to release the old ways completely. A new generation of thoughts and attitudes had to grow up within me and the old attitudes had to die away, before I could find that life of serenity and sobriety that I so desperately wanted. I finally found that life and am enjoying it today.

The Israelites spent the next forty years living in the wilderness just outside Canaan, until that old generation had died. Moses was taken to the top of a mountain and God showed him the promised land, but he never entered it. He too died in the wilderness. But during that time a new generation was growing, a generation who would never cry for the fleshpots of Egypt or ask why. The new generation would make mistakes but would never lose faith in God. Moreover, this new generation would be led by a man who had never doubted, moaned, or even complained. His name was Joshua, captain of the army. He would lead them with a clear vision and resolve. And this new generation would follow with conviction, and with the trust that was so badly lacking a generation ago, that God would lead them to victory over their enemies and give to them the promised land.

Exercises

1. Do you waste your time in self-pity? In times when you are prone to feel sorry for yourself, ask, "What good will come out of feeling this way? What good feelings am I blocking?"

2. What destructive part of you must die before a new and healthy you can be born? Visualize what life would be like without that destructive part of you. Imagine God filling in the missing part with its opposite virtue. Does it become easier to leave behind?

3. Begin a prayer to God asking him to lead you not where you want to go, but where he wants you to. Ask for the power to follow. Does your spiritual direction become more evident to you? Are you better able to follow?

READINGS

After the death of Moses, the servant of the Lord, it came to pass that the Lord spoke to Joshua the son of Nun, Moses' assistant, saying: "Moses my servant is dead. Now therefore, arise, go over this Jordan, you and all this people, to the land which I am giving to them. . . . Only be strong and very courageous, that you may observe to do according to all the law which Moses my servant commanded you; do not turn from it to the right hand or to the left, that you may prosper wherever you go. Joshua 1:1-2, 7

Now Jericho was securely shut up because of the children of Israel; none went out and none came in. And the Lord said to Joshua: "See! I have given Jericho into your hand, its king, and the mighty men of valor. You shall march around the city, all you men of war; you shall go all around the city once. This you shall do six days. And seven priests shall bear seven trumpets of rams' horns before the ark. But the seventh day you shall march around the city seven times, and the priests shall blow the trumpets. Then it shall come to pass, when they make a long blast with the ram's horn, and when you hear the sound of the trumpet, that all the people shall shout with a great shout; then the wall of the city will fall down flat. And the people shall go up every man straight before him."   Joshua 6:1-5

So the people shouted when the priests blew the trumpets. And it happened when the people heard the sound of the trumpet, and the people shouted with a great shout, that the wall fell down flat. Then the people went straight up into the city, every man straight before him, and they took the city. And they utterly destroyed all that was in the city. . . . So the Lord was with Joshua, and his fame spread throughout the country.   Joshua 6:20, 27

CHAPTER NINE

Conquering Spiritual Foes

Jericho

The walls of Jericho symbolize the falsities which defend evils.

Arcana Coelestia 8815

A New Attitude

Forty years later, the new generation, raised in the wilderness on the bread and water of God, had come of age. Moses and the original Israelites who refused to enter the land were now dead. It was at this point that God spoke to Joshua, saying, "Moses my servant is dead. Now therefore arise, go over this Jordan, you and all the people, to the land which I am giving to them—the children of Israel. Every place that the sole of your foot will tread upon I have given you. . . . No man shall be able to stand before you all the days of your life; as I was with Moses, so I will be with you. I will not leave you nor forsake you. Be strong and of good courage, for to this people you shall divide as an inheritance the land which I swore to their fathers to give them" (Joshua 1:2-6). God promised Joshua and Israel that he would never leave them; but he said they must be strong, courageous, trusting, and willing to follow what he says, in order to be victorious over their enemies and inherit the promised land.

The old generation probably would have said, "We don't want the land!" Or perhaps they would have mumbled that they wished they were back in Egypt. But this was a new generation, who didn't do or say any of these things. The new generation plainly said, "All that you command us we will do, and wherever you send us we will go" (Joshua 1:16). These people were ready to follow God and take the land, no questions asked.

Spiritually, the second generation symbolizes the new attitude we can develop so that we can cross over into a new and spiritual state of life. Sometimes it is so difficult for us to let go and follow God. Sometimes we want to do things our way, without God. And, as we have seen previously, it leads us toward feeling stuck in a wasteland. But we can learn to think and act in a new way. Like this new generation, we can learn to say, "All that you command us to do we will do, and wherever you send us we will go." This attitude makes life less complicated. Instead of worrying about work, bills, taxes, marriage, kids, the car, insurance, health, life in general, and trying to manage all these complications of life without any spiritual help, we simply start our day by asking the Divine to lead us and to help us cope with our daily tasks. We pray that God reveals his will and gives us the power to carry it out. Instead of trying half measures to lead us out of our state of spiritual apathy and confusion, we ask God for direction, and we become willing to follow that direction. We keep it that simple, and the problems of life really do become manageable and workable. We find ourselves able to move forward, out of a spiritual wasteland, toward a life of genuine spirituality.

Crossing Over

When Israel crossed over into the new land, the Ark of the Covenant, carried by the priests, led the way. As soon as the priests' feet touched the Jordan river, the waters parted, and they crossed over on dry land. When they entered the promised land, we are told, the manna ceased. The Israelites no longer had to eat the bread of the wilderness but could now enjoy the fruit of the land, any and every time they wanted it.

This is the second boundary or barrier of water that their God parted. What is the difference between the first boundary of the Red Sea and this one? These two boundaries represent spiritual divisions in the types of mental states we must cross in our journey toward spirituality. Crossing the Red Sea represented being freed from bondage, from the slavery of our destructive inclination. It is what the theologians call our "repentance," turning from evil. Crossing that boundary, we found ourselves on an uncharted journey, in a dry and thirsty search for truth and the meaning of life. This stage is called "reformation," where we "re-form," or in modern terms, we "get our act together." Now, in this later stage of spiritual development, we cross a new border, represented by the Jordan River, which ends the wilderness search and introduces a truly meaningful, spiritual, and flourishing way of life. This new process is called "regeneration," the process of being reborn. Many obstacles still block our way, and many spiritual battles will need to be fought to make that life completely our own; but we definitely leave behind the desert search for answers. A new process takes place as we claim for ourselves a home and a land we can truly call our own.

The Ark of the Covenant's leading the way across the Jordan represents what must lead us in our journey into a new life. The ark contained the Ten Commandments. If these basic and simple rules of God and man are made the priority in our lives, they will lead into the promised land. Again, listen to God's words of advice to Joshua and Israel: "This book of the law shall not depart from your mouth, but you shall meditate in it day and night, that you may observe to do according to all that is written in it. For then you will make your way prosperous, and then you will have good success" (Joshua 1:8). To the degree that we are able to love our God with all our heart and our neighbor as ourself, which is the crux of the Ten Commandments, we will leave that life of emptiness behind in favor of a new life full of limitless possibilities.

Remember that when the Israelites stood in front of the Red Sea, Moses told the people to move forward. That symbolized how we should move forward and actually try to live a better life if we want one. We can't change our lives if we just stand there thinking about it or worrying about it. The same is represented in this instance, but the literal imagery is even more appropriate. As soon as the priests, who carried the ark, touched the waters of the Jordan with their feet, the river parted. Can the biblical imagery here become any clearer? If we want to change, we've got to move forward. Like the priests, we've got to get our feet wet trying to lead a new life. If we just get our feet wet trying, the obstruction parts and we cross over into a new state.

As already mentioned, when the Israelites finally crossed over, the manna ceased. They wouldn't need manna because they were able to enjoy the fruits of the land. Spiritually, at this point in our journey toward recovery, no longer do we enjoy only a mild sense of spiritual delight, but the real and delicious fruits of a new and beautiful life. We enjoy the perceptible delights that a loving and spiritual life brings.

For instance, maybe early in our efforts we tried to be a more loving person to those around us. At first, the satisfaction of doing so was hardly perceptible; nobody seemed to notice. We didn't feel any great reward for our attempt at change, only a slight sense of fulfillment. But a time comes when the slight sense of fulfillment can become perceptible joy. We can recognize that people begin to respond differently, more positively, to us. They become much warmer and open because of our new attitude toward them. We may also inwardly sense a joy in showing our love and concern toward our fellow humans. We derive a wonderful sense of being useful, worthy, and alive; and can begin to enjoy the real fruits of a new life. This is just one example of how the fruits can come. We still have a long way to go to claim that new life for our own; but the fruits appear, and we taste their sweet and life-refreshing sustenance.

Jericho

Although the Israelites had crossed over into Canaan, they had a long way to go before this land could be called their own. Many enemies blocked their way. One of the strongest lived behind the protective wall of Jericho. This wall was so large and so wide that people even built houses on top of it. Jericho was the first enemy city Israel would challenge in the new land; it looked well fortified, strong, impenetrable. The Israelites had their work cut out for them.

Jericho, as the first enemy blocking Israel from its inheritance, symbolizes a deeply rooted character defect or destructive tendency that blocks us from our spiritual inheritance. The enemy within Jericho's walls symbolizes a well-protected but evil character defect like greed, contempt, jealousy—a real spiritual enemy. This enemy is strongly protected by the walls of denial that prevent us from removing it from our lives.

Earlier, when we saw that God instructed Moses to get water from a rock, we discussed how rocks symbolize facts or knowledge. These facts can be used for either good or evil purposes. In the symbolism of the wall of Jericho, facts or fragments of knowledge piled one on top of the other to build a wall of lies. What is a lie, except a fact used in the wrong way, to hide and protect something evil? Pile a bunch of lies together and you create a very strong wall of denial to protect the internal defect from discovery and removal. On our spiritual journey, we reach a point when we are ready to attack that defect and remove it, but we've subconsciously built so many walls of denial around it for so long that it doesn't go away easily.

Pick any character defect and you can see the walls people build around it. Those who suffer from addiction have subconsciously piled lies on top of one another to protect themselves from changing. Here are a few of those stones:

"I don't drink any more than anyone else."

"It's my life. I can do what I want."

"It's the only friend I have."

"My life has been miserable, so I deserve to have a good time now and then."

"It helps me cope."

"It takes the edge off the day."

"She made me this way. It's her fault I drink."

"I can't help it. It runs in the family."

There are hundreds more, which can create a tremendous wall of denial to hide the problem.

Another example can be found in the realm of jealousy and resentment. People who hang onto those destructive feelings also have their stones piled on top of one another to protect them:

"Why do I never get what I deserve?"

"I'm better than she is, but she stole the show as usual."

"These idiots are way off base, but they won't listen to me. Fools."

"I could have been promoted if I had catered to the boss as he did, but that's beneath me."

"The only way he could beat me was by cheating."

"That should be me getting the praise. I was robbed."

"I deserve to be angry!"

These statements pile up in the mind of the jealous and resentful person, surrounding the defect, giving it credibility, protection, a safe place to dwell within.

Look at some greedy ideas in business today and the walls they've created. A ruthless business executive tells an employee, "You've got to be heartless in this business. Don't think about the other guy. Kill or be killed. Don't feel sorry for him; that could be you. You've got to lie, cheat and steal to get ahead in this business. The rule out here is the strongest survive." These lies, piled one on top of another, have become that executive's wall to protect his depraved nature. The destructive tendencies or evils flourish behind it.

Instead of wasting our energy in digging out the faults of others or in raging against the injustice of the world, each of us should ask ourselves a few basic questions: "What are the personal Jerichos in my life? What character defects have I been protecting behind my own wall of lies? Do I want to remove these defects? How will I get busy removing them?"

The Israelites sent spies into Jericho to discover its weaknesses, which symbolizes a self-search for those deeply fortified defects, to see what they are, where they are and how to remove them. This is self-examination, a personal inventory that is essential to calculate the scope and magnitude of our defects and determine how we might begin to remove them.

When you discover a strong destructive tendency within yourself, you must spy on it before doing battle with it. Analyze it; look for its weak spots to see how you might best attack the wall of defense. For instance, if you suffer from jealousy, you can't just decide not to be jealous anymore and expect that problem to simply go away. You should explore this defect by asking, "When do I get jealous? Are there certain actions of others that start the negative feeling within me? What am I missing that I feel compelled to be jealous of others? What are the lies I've been telling myself?" Only when you search out that particular enemy and learn about it can you do battle with it and claim victory.

Maybe your Jericho is that you are possessive and controlling of others. You need to look closely at the problem before you confront it head on. Ask yourself, "Why am I so possessive? What am I afraid of?" Feel the walls of your destructive tendency. Ask yourself, "Is there a lie or series of lies I've told myself to make me cling to my partner or friends?" Examine the defect in order to plan your assault against it.

I know, for me, the desire to control was one spiritual enemy I wanted to know well before taking it head on. Instead of trying not to control situations, I had to explore the whole issue of control. When did I feel like controlling? What circumstances brought this tendency into the open? Were there certain people who pushed my buttons about this issue? Was it a childhood wound that caused me to want to control? Were some methods of control okay in certain circumstances? Asking these questions helped me to prepare to do battle with my control issues; I knew the enemy well before confronting it.

Commander of God's Army

Right in the middle of the story about Jericho, a fascinating little narrative is inserted that doesn't seem to fit at first (Joshua 5:13-15). Just before Joshua leaves to fight the people of Jericho, he is walking along alone, surveying the land near the city. He looks up and is stunned to see a man standing in front of him with his sword drawn in his hand. He asks the man, "Are you for us or for our adversaries?" The man answers, "No, but as commander of the army of the Lord I have now come." Joshua asks him, "What does my Lord say to his servant?" The angel replies, "Take the sandal off your foot, for the place where you stand is holy."

That's it. The next verse returns to Jericho, and then the narrative appears to change, with God giving Joshua final instructions about how to take the city. Some biblical commentaries say that the rest of the story must have been lost, because the commander was obviously going to tell Joshua more but didn't; or the angel is an emissary conveying God's battleplan. But perhaps what the angel said wasn't as important as what he stood for. And that is the key to this story. For the angel's presence alone gave a strong, symbolic message, which needs no further dialogue. The appearance of the commander of God's army, with sword drawn, symbolizes the divine help Joshua would receive to defeat Jericho—it cries out that Joshua would not be alone, that legions of angels would help fight against Jericho. In truth, Joshua and his insignificant men could never beat this monster of a city. But God and his holy angels could; they could break any walls down, no matter how thick, and vanquish the most formidable foe.

The same symbol stands true for us. When we meet our inner enemies, if left to our own resources, we wouldn't even know where to begin. We are powerless against our destructive tendencies. The walls are too high, the enemies' power too great, their savagery beyond anything we have ever dealt with. But we are not alone. It is God who fights these battles for us. It is a power greater than self that brings those walls of denial down and crushes the enemy. And I believe the angels take part in those battles to protect us. Angels watch over us and help moderate our thoughts. When destructive thoughts enter, the angels are there to combat against them. They do so with thoughts of the Divine, of showing a different way, of instilling feelings of peace and contentment. Like the angel who appeared to Joshua, angels stand ready to help us in our spiritual battles. As Psalm 91:11 tells us, "He shall give his angels charge over you to keep you in all your ways."

The City Falls

The children of Israel, at God's command, didn't immediately attack Jericho. The first time they left their camp, they marched in procession, blowing their trumpets, with the priests carrying the ark in front of them. They circled Jericho once, then returned to their camp. They did this each day for six days. They came out early and silently, except for the priests' trumpets blowing, marched around the walled city, then disappeared again until the next morning. Imagine the fear, stress, and panic that engulfed the inhabitants of Jericho who witnessed this odd sight each morning. The rhythm of marching and the blaring of trumpets must have created a crushing anticipation for a battle that never seemed to come. When would these strangers attack?

On the seventh day the Israelites marched around Jericho seven times. Then the priests sounded their trumpets, and Joshua commanded the people, "Shout, for the Lord has given you the city!" (Joshua 6:16) The Israelites obeyed and the walls of Jericho crumbled at their shouts. With the fortification destroyed, the Israelites entered the city and took it swiftly.

The Israelites' approach has some important symbolic lessons for us. They didn't attack the city immediately but marched around it once for six days in a row. At the least their tactics struck fear into the people of the city. But the number six offers some clues that reveal what their tactics could mean symbolically. Where else is the number six significant in the Bible? One of the Ten Commandments says that we should labor for six days and rest on the seventh. Also, the world was created in six days, as we are told in Exodus 20:11: "In six days God created the heavens and the earth, the sea, and all that is in them, and rested on the seventh day." In the language of the Bible, the number six symbolizes a progression of growth, culminating in a seventh day of rest.

The same is represented by the number six in the Jericho story. Six represents a progression. We don't discover a strongly barricaded defect within us and just snap our fingers to wipe it out. Only a progression of time and effort can destroy it, as represented by the command to labor for six days. Any strong defect of character that is heavily guarded by denial is going to demand time and effort before those walls can be knocked down and the core of the problem confronted. It's not going to happen in one day. To tackle resentment, fear, anger, or any deeply rooted character defect takes persistence and determination. We have to be steadfast, confront the problem daily and regularly, even as Israel marched around that wall daily and regularly for six days.

There is an important lesson here: don't give up! A lot of people try to change their lives in one day or overnight. Some people spend one or two days fighting a particular defect, become discouraged, and quit. They tire of marching around their personal Jericho, wondering why the walls aren't falling down yet. It takes time! Twelve-step groups say, "Practice spiritual progress, not perfection." Keep up the work. Take life one day at a time, one march around Jericho at a time, and changes will occur. In the long run, the walls begin to crumble and real changes can then take place. But you must be patient and follow God's command. March around that city one day at a time, and let God knock the walls down! He will, when you are ready.

As the Israelites marched around Jericho, the priests continually blew trumpets. On the last day, after marching around seven times, the priests blew the trumpets and the people shouted. As a result, the walls fell down. People have long interpreted blowing the trumpet as symbolic of proclaiming the truth. Throughout the Bible, blowing trumpets symbolize such a proclamation. In Isaiah 58:1, we read, "Cry aloud, spare not; lift up your voice like a trumpet; tell my people their transgressions." In Ezekiel 33:4-5, the prophets are compared to watchmen who should "blow the trumpets," that is, warn the people when evil arises. We are told, "Whoever hears the sound of the trumpet and does not take warning, if the sword comes and takes him away, his blood shall be on his own head." And in Rev. 1:10-11, when the risen Christ speaks to John on the Isle of Patmos, John says, "I heard behind me a loud voice, as of a trumpet, saying, 'I am the Alpha and the Omega, the First and the Last.'"

On a spiritual level, to march around Jericho blowing the trumpets is to confront a defect of character with the plain truth. Proclaiming the truth about our character flaws consistently and regularly in our own minds will bring those otherwise impenetrable walls down. Only the truth we know can help us knock down the walls of denial we have built around the defect we are battling.

Does that sound simplistic? It really isn't. Think about a defect you might suffer from. Perhaps it expresses itself in jealousy and resentment of others. Blowing the trumpet around that well-fortified defect would be continually reminding you, "Live and let live," or "Forgive and you will be forgiven," or "Do unto others as you would have them do unto you," and other axioms that directly confront your jealousy and the lies built around it. To blow that mental trumpet regularly when the jealousy emerges will begin to have an effect. The truth has a special power to break those walls down, but it takes persistence. The Israelites blew those trumpets for days on end; but the seventh day finally came and the walls of Jericho fell down. Ours will fall as well.

A woman's Jericho may be a tremendous lack of trust in God, the walls of which consist of half-truths and lies that say God is powerless to help her or doesn't care about her; or perhaps that there is no God at all. The trumpets she must blow should proclaim

God's presence. She must remind herself that she isn't alone, that God does care for her deeply and will always lead her in good times and in bad toward a loving and fulfilling relationship with him. She must proclaim the truth to herself regularly, especially in times of fear and lack of trust in God. Eventually the heavily encrusted lies that prevent her from seeing spiritual reality will begin to crack and crumble away. Mistrust, once exposed, loses its power and is easily vanquished.

One of my personal Jerichos, a deeply rooted character defect, is viewing people who don't agree with me as "the enemy." The walls that protect this defect are lies that tell me that I am right and those who oppose me are wrong, that differing opinions will lead to hurt and failure, that when people disagree with me they are personally attacking my character. To break this defect down, I have to remind myself that I'm not always right and others are not always wrong. In times of discord with others I have to blow that inward trumpet at my defect, proclaiming to myself that, just because people disagree with me, they are not my enemies; they are not wrong but simply see things differently; they have a right to their opinions. Sometimes I have to *shout* inwardly to penetrate the walls of denial and rid my life of this Jericho of mine.

It is significant that the blowing of the trumpets on the seventh day was followed by the Israelites' giving a mighty shout. This is a vigorous affirmation of the truth, a conclusive "Amen!" in which we triumphantly acknowledge that this indeed is the truth. We can say, "It is so!" We affirm the truth proclaimed in our minds. We say, "It is so: I do not have to be jealous! I must live and let live! I understand that now!" "It is so: God is trustworthy! I believe that now!" "It is so: people who disagree with me are not my enemy!" This is what is meant by the answering shout of Israel: affirming the truth of the trumpets, proclaiming our belief in the truth and confirming it with an inward shout.

Another way to look at the significance of this inward shouting is to see it as a cry to God. It symbolizes our calling out to God for help. When Jesus rode into Jerusalem as if an earthly king, the people shouted, "Hosanna." The word *hosanna* means "save us now!" The people could not be silenced. Even if they were forced into silence, it is written that "the very stones would cry out!" There is something in us that yearns to cry out, to lift up our voices, to acknowledge God's power, and to ask for his help.

When we've blown our trumpets consistently at our personal failing, we can let it all go and cry out to our God, "Save us now, O God! Save us from this enemy!" Many people, in discussing their spiritual lives, have told me that they did not receive help until they reached a point of desperation over a certain problem, defect, or compulsion and truly cried out to God. After that final cry, the walls of illusion and denial came tumbling down, and that problem soon began to be manageable and dissolve away.

God promises that those walls will come tumbling down. We can see them fall, too. It can be an awesome sight. Suddenly we can see what we never saw before—the truth about our life. We might say to ourselves, "Was I really like that all those years?" We then know well what the answer is and what we must now do. The illusion is gone. We recognize, "I don't have to be possessive anymore," or "I don't have to judge others," or "I can easily live and let live, now that I clearly see what has been bugging me." The walls are gone. The defect of character, disgusting as it is, stands there naked, vulnerable, and powerless over us. Victory is ours.

After the walls fell down, the children of Israel entered and wiped out that city. Only a few people who helped them were spared. The rest were destroyed and the city was burned. Historically, such cruel takeovers were not unusual. Also, as we have seen earlier, Israel wiped out the enemy so as not to be perverted by their immoral practices. Spiritually, the lesson is one that cannot be overstated: we must wipe out that hideous evil completely. Once we expose the defect, we must show no leniency. It never did us any favors, and it never will. When the walls of illusion crumble, it's time to destroy those defects before they re-arm and destroy us. Knock them out with the sword of truth and annihilate them. Not until then will there be peace.

That's conquering Jericho. It symbolizes the first real victory over a deeply rooted defect. For most of us, there are many Jerichos, or at least similar strongly fortified cities in this land whose walls must be broken down. This first victory signifies the tremendous progress we can now make in life. With a little trust in God, miracles can happen. Huge walls can crumble. Inner enemies so long hidden from our view are now exposed, and with God's help, we can overcome them.

In my work as a minister and a counselor, I have seen people beat the big ones in their lives. I have seen a young man conquer a major sex problem; an older woman beat loneliness and depression; couples overcome the enemy of mutual neglect and self-centeredness; people beat addictions to chemicals, sex, work habits, food, and unhealthy relationships. As the walls crumble around the inner enemy, that enemy is exposed and is removed. The relief, the sense of deeper order to life, of healing, of celebration in victory is real for these people.

The tremendous victory over our spiritual enemies helps us to carve out a firm foothold in this new and glorious land. As we savor our victory and anticipate claiming all of our spiritual inheritance, God's words from Joshua 1:9 ring out in our minds and hearts, filling us with pure joy: "Be strong and of good courage, do not be afraid, nor be dismayed, for the Lord your God is with you, wherever you go." For perhaps the first time in our lives, we know that his words are true.

Exercises

1. In times of spiritual confusion, stop what you are doing and ask God to lead you. Repeat this phrase: "Whatever you command me to do I will do, and wherever you tell me to go I will go."

2. Sit down and reflect. Is there a Jericho in your life? Write down the denials that protect that defect. How can you begin to break those walls down?

3. If you've discovered a Jericho in your life, what true statements can you use as a trumpet to weaken its walls? Write down three or four statements that directly address your problem. (For instance, if your Jericho is some sort of fear, write three or four statements that confront that fear, such as "No matter where I go, God is with me; I have nothing to fear but fear itself; I am in God's hand now and always," etc.). Use these regularly to combat that Jericho. And don't forget that inward shout!

READINGS

But the children of Israel committed a trespass regarding the accursed things, for Achan . . . took of the accursed things. . . . Now Joshua sent men from Jericho to Ai. . . . And they returned to Joshua and said to him, "Do not let all the people go up, but let about two or three thousand men go up and attack Ai . . . for the people of Ai are few." So about three thousand men went up there from the people, but they fled before the men of Ai. And the men of Ai struck down about thirty-six men, for they chased them. . . . Then Joshua tore his clothes, and fell to the earth on his face before the ark of the Lord until evening. . . . So the Lord said to Joshua: "Get up! Why do you lie thus on your face? Israel has sinned. . . . For they have even taken some of the accursed things. . . . Neither will I be with you anymore, unless you destroy the accursed from among you.". . . So Joshua rose early in the morning and brought Israel by their tribes, and the tribe of Judah was taken. . . . Then he brought his household man by man, and Achan . . . was taken. . . . So Joshua sent messengers, and they ran to [Achan's] tent; and there it was, hidden in his tent.   Joshua 7 ff.

Then the Lord said to Joshua; "Do not be afraid. . . . Lay an ambush for the city behind it.". . . So he took about five thousand men and set them in ambush. . . . Joshua went that night into the midst of the valley. Now it happened, when the king of Ai saw it, that the men of the city hastened and rose early and went out against Israel to battle. . . . But he did not know that there was an ambush against him behind the city. . . . So those in ambush rose quickly out of their place . . . and they entered the city and took it, and hastened to set the city on fire. And when the men of Ai looked behind them, they saw . . . so that they had no power to flee this way or that way. . . . And they struck them down, so that they let none of them escape. Joshua 8 ff.

CHAPTER TEN

Minor Challenges

Ai

Real repentance is examining oneself, recognizing and acknowledging one's sins, appealing to the Lord and beginning a new life.

True Christian Religion 528

Achan's Sin

The Israelites had just won a glorious victory over Jericho. They had triumphed in their first battle for the promised land. They had followed God's directions, the walls fell, and they easily conquered the city. They were very confident that they could now conquer the rest of their enemies.

But in reality, all was not completely well. They had been told not to take the "accursed things," certain spoils of Jericho, which were considered profane if taken for personal use. But one Israelite named Achan had secretly disobeyed and had taken a Babylonian garment, two hundred shekels of silver, a wedge of gold—all forbidden spoils of war. Achan's action would curse Israel as they moved forward to attack the next enemy stronghold.

The next city, a fortress called Ai, was not as large as Jericho. Spies returned from their mission to say, "There's no reason to bring everyone along. The inhabitants of the city are few. Take a couple of thousand men along and we'll capture it in no time." The Israelites confidently rushed forward to attack Ai, and they were surprisingly defeated. They fled before the people of Ai and regrouped many miles away. Their hearts melted from fear and utter bewilderment. Joshua, in total humiliation, fell on his face and prayed to God for an answer. Why had they been beaten, he wondered. What was wrong? The Lord answered him: Israel had not fully obeyed. Someone had taken of the accursed things, and Israel must find out whom and destroy him and the accursed things. So Joshua thoroughly searched all the tribes of Israel and eventually found Achan. Achan confessed. He and all that was his were destroyed, and Israel became free of what has been called "Achan's Sin."

Now the Israelites were ready to claim victory over Ai. But this time they asked their God how to attack this enemy. God gave them a brilliant battle plan, and Israel defeated Ai and utterly destroyed it. The enemy, who had at first defeated Israel, was vanquished. The Israelites thanked their God for the great victory they had been given, and they renewed their covenant with the Divine. They expected more battles; but, with God on their side, victory was a certainty.

Spiritual Setbacks

Like Israel, we suffer temporary setbacks in our efforts to rid ourselves of our spiritual enemies. In the beginning we have success, and sometimes, as with the Israelites, we can celebrate a tremendous victory over a gigantic and powerful enemy in our lives. Some character defect, represented by Jericho, seems to fall before us into dust and ashes. We take on a powerful character defect, shortcoming, compulsive thought or behavior, and, with God on our side, we knock it down and run right over it. But then what can happen? Like Israel, we beat the big ones; but when we try to rid ourselves of the less significant defects of character, represented by Ai, they seem to chase us all over the place and beat us badly.

Have you ever experienced this? You have a minor shortcoming that can be easily corrected, and you take some halfhearted steps to remove it, thinking it will easily fall. Like Joshua sending only a few thousand men to beat the enemy, you give the problem half your attention, half an effort to overcome it. But what happens? As soon as you focus on it, it becomes twice as bad, twice as powerful and vicious. Instead of wiping it out, you find yourself in fear of it, running from it, wondering how this ever got to be such a problem.

Perhaps you think you have a small problem with swearing or telling dirty jokes. That doesn't seem too harmful, does it? Many problems are worse! But what happens when you try to stop? For some, this is when every other word becomes vulgar, and inappropriate jokes suddenly return in every conversation. Or perhaps you've decided not to gossip. That's not necessarily the worst habit you have. At least you didn't think so, until you tried to stop. Suddenly you find yourself talking about other people and their problems behind their backs in every conversation you have. You wonder why this problem has grown so big. You never realized how vicious this defect could be. You thought you could easily beat it, but it chases you all over the place. You can worry that if you can't beat these insignificant shortcomings, you will never conquer the more significant ones. Like Joshua, you can find yourself groveling on the ground, feeling sorry for yourself, and asking God, "Why me?"

One of the many reasons that these little defects are so difficult to handle is that we don't take the shortcoming seriously. Like Israel, we don't think we need to send in all the troops. Half measures, though, will get us nowhere. If we aren't completely willing to let go of those defects, they don't go away; they become worse. We have to become entirely ready to have God remove these defects of character. We need to focus on them with all our attention, use our best effort to beat them, and be willing to let God lead us.

The Israelites' other mistake was not heeding the counsel of God. It is amazing how quickly they forgot how their God had given them their last victorious battle plan, how he made the walls of Jericho fall down. But when it came to moving on to engage the next enemy, God was unquestionably absent from their plans. Sometimes we act the same way. After real spiritual progress, especially in the beginning, individuals can forget all the help they received from God. They can start to think that they actually did remove that defect by themselves, that they are super-warriors against evil and corruption, that nothing can hold them down. But when people forget God, they also forget to ask for divine power and his wisdom to guide them. The result is spiritual defeat. As soon as they meet their next character defect, regardless of its lack of size or ferocity, they suffer defeat. They can't do it without God. Sometimes, like Israel, they have to learn the hard way.

My good friend Andrew once told me how little trouble he had giving up drinking, once he realized that, as an alcoholic, he was powerless over alcohol. When he finally hit bottom, he knew that only God could overcome this addiction for him, that he couldn't do it himself. With that recognition and trust in God, the walls of denial came tumbling down, and he, through the grace of God, soundly defeated his addiction. But if drinking was his Jericho, smoking was his Ai. He said that even though he had quit drinking so easily, it took him years and years to quit smoking. For one thing, he couldn't see the immediate negative effects, and so he had less incentive to quit. But the most fundamental reason was that he refused to let God do it. Every time Andrew got ready to quit, he would brace for the chilling first few days without nicotine. He would clench his fists, get ready to hold on and ride out the withdrawals. It was impossible. He even tried a variety of techniques like self-hypnosis and nicotine gum. He tried to conquer this habit himself, under his own power. He said that he found himself wondering, disappointed, a cigarette in the mouth, why it was so easy to quit the booze but not the cigarettes.

Finally it came to him. When he decided to quit drinking, he simply turned it over completely to God. He realized that to quit smoking he would have to do the same. He finally did: he fully conceded that he had no power whatsoever over his problem of smoking and that God would not only have to do it for him, but would have to show him how. That didn't mean Andrew shouldn't act in cooperation with God to remove this enemy; it meant that his own strength, power, and wit had nothing to do with winning the battle. He simply had to come to the full recognition that God would do it all. With that attitude, Andrew quit and never returned to smoking. He also said that after at least a dozen of the most painful attempts to quit on his own, this final assault on smoking was not only painless but even pleasant! He said, "This new 'turning-it-over-to-God' to quit something as silly as smoking became a spiritual experience. I found him in a new way."

Smoking isn't a great spiritual sin, but it is a destructive habit that can stand before us as a formidable foe. Many people have found that, until they took their smoking habit seriously and looked for some sort of higher power to help, they were unable to overcome this addiction. This is true not only with smoking, but with all habits, defects of character, and even the more deep-seated tendencies toward evil we may find implanted within our character.

The Accursed Things

There is another reason that we are unable to beat certain shortcomings. This reason doesn't have much to do with those shortcomings themselves, but with the other shortcomings we dealt with before engaging a new one. Sometimes it is difficult to battle certain character defects because we hold onto others. Those other defects come back to haunt us and prevent us from making progress.

This is illustrated in the story of Achan holding onto the accursed things, the spoils of Jericho. The Israelites were told to wipe out everything in Jericho and take nothing for themselves. This symbolizes God's instructions to wipe out completely any character defect we decide to fight. We can't let any part of it live; if we hold onto it, it will, so to speak, curse us. Achan's taking of the accursed things, and Israel's subsequently losing the next battle, symbolizes just that. If we hold onto some of the pleasure of one defect of character, that same defect will resurface when we work on another, and it will prevent us from winning future battles. If we take the accursed treasures of Jericho, we will not be able to defeat Ai.

Like Achan, sometimes people do hold onto the treasures of their spiritual enemies. Individuals can want to wipe out a dominant spiritual enemy such as anger, jealousy, or lust; but they can be tempted to hold onto the treasures that lie at the center of those defects. Those enemy treasures are the pleasures those defects bring, the payoffs for holding onto them. They are sick delights, a sense of self-righteousness perhaps, a feeling of great power and control, a rush of excitement and immediate pleasure. But like the spoils of Jericho, these outwardly beautiful treasures are cursed and will hurt if they are held onto. God warns individuals not to hold onto them after they defeat a character defect. But like Achan, sometimes it is hard to listen and obey. It is a temptation to hold onto some of the inner pleasure these dysfunctional behaviors carry with them. They can be seen as special treasures to be hidden away and enjoyed later on.

As an illustration, let's talk about anger, a trait most of us have a problem with at one time or another. Perhaps we have been working on this one for a while. Let's say we finally win the battle to stop venting our anger at people. We stop lashing out at our family, friends, or people at work. That is the Jericho that falls before us as we really do make progress. But at the same time we may not completely let go of the *feelings* of anger itself. Like the forbidden treasures of Jericho, those feelings are alluring. They seem to give us a sense of esteem, a feeling of self-righteousness. So we may defeat the destructive tendency of venting that anger, but we don't really get rid of the anger itself. Like Achan, we may recognize that it is forbidden treasure, but it's so appealing. We secretly hold onto it.

The problem with this is that, when we move on to get rid of another defect of character, the anger within can prevent us from

success. For instance, the new spiritual enemy we choose to conquer may be our impatience. Maybe it has never been too much of
a problem before. Like Ai, we consider it a small obstacle that
shouldn't take too much effort to overcome. All we have to do is
learn to keep calm, let time pass, give people a chance. But if even
a bit of anger lies hidden within the inner chambers of our mind, it
will surface as we fight to overcome impatience. Like Achan's treasure, it will curse us. As soon as someone doesn't do exactly what
we want, we find ourselves boiling with an overwhelming sense of
intolerance. If our child is clumsy with an item dear to us, we can
feel the anger within suddenly emerge and we lash out. If a friend
is late or traffic holds us up, we become indignant and intolerant.
"What's happening?" we ask ourselves, "Why can't I be more
patient?" Even though we may have totally ceased to snap at people or yell at those close to us, we can't seem to beat the defect of
impatience. The anger, the accursed things that we secretly hold
onto, blocks our progress.

Consider another example. We may have a quiet tendency to
control and manipulate our partner. We may have learned to subtly reward the actions we like and subtly punish those we do not.
(Fellow manipulators know what I mean.) But perhaps we fight
against this quiet manipulation and defeat it. We stop the subtle
rewards and punishments. But, at the same time, we may not completely remove all feelings underlying our clandestine control.
Deep within lies possessiveness, selfishness. These feelings give us
a sense of being in control, a twisted sense of fulfillment and security. We may hold onto these feelings as treasures. The entire
enemy of quiet control has not been destroyed. Outwardly, the
action has ceased; inwardly the destructive tendency sits deeply
hidden and smolders, ready to flare up again at a later date.

The problem is that it does flare up. For instance, we may later
decide to work on our honesty and openness with people, to put on
less pretense about who we are, to show our real self. But the first
time we try this with our spouse, we somehow openly shower that

spouse with words of contempt. We don't quietly manipulate anymore. We just complain and bicker. We wonder why our new
attempt to show our true self sours. The reason is that we never
completely annihilated our first problem, and it halts our progress.

Another example of holding on, with detrimental results, can be
seen in the man who is trying to clean up his act sexually. Perhaps
he has won the battle over lewdness, a fascination with pornogra-
phy, and sex without love or commitment. He has changed his life,
has stopped his sexual excesses, and believes that he has turned over
a new leaf. He just fantasizes instead. He stops the action, but holds
onto the accursed delight.

But when he finally does find a woman he cares about, he won't
be able to shake his old ways. He'll try to love, to be unselfish, to
care about his new mate; but his sexual fantasies will emerge and
preclude a loving relationship. Not until he cleans up his act completely and gets rid of not only the lewd actions but the lewd
thoughts and subsequent delights will he be able truly to love a
woman. He's got to find the accursed things and destroy them.

This is true with all of the spiritual problems or obstacles we
face. If we find a problem that we cannot overcome, we have to ask
ourselves and our God, "What is the problem? What holds me back
from making progress?" Joshua asks God for the answer, and God
says that someone has taken the accursed things and instructs
Joshua to search out the entire camp, find them and those who have
taken them. In our lives, we too must find what we have held onto
that prevents us from spiritual success. We cannot reach up with
open hands to receive new life, while clinging to the accursed things
of the past.

If we discover a lack of patience, we must sit down to reflect and
trace its origins. If we can't communicate with our spouse, is the
problem a result of a deeper defect of character that we continue
to hold onto? If we suffer in our effort to truly love our partner, is
it because we have taken a wrong approach to members of the
opposite sex? It may not be easy to find the answer. Like the

Israelites, we must search through our own camp, take a personal inventory, in order to find the problem. Joshua interrogated one tribe at a time, one family at a time, one person at a time to find the culprit. We, in effect, can do the same. We look at the different facets of our lives and try to discover the culprit that holds us back. For instance, the man dealing with his inability to love his partner has got to sit down and sort it out in his mind. He has to go through the different categories of his life, even as Joshua went through the different tribes, until he finds the culprit. His conversation with himself may run something like this: "Is it an inability to listen that stops me from being loving? No, I listen. Is it some need I feel is not being filled that makes me unloving? Perhaps. What about our communication? That seems good. Where do I find my greatest problem giving? Is it of a sexual nature? Well, yes. It does have to do with that. In fact, that's it, I think . . ." From there he must explore exactly what he's been holding onto and get rid of it.

By refusing to release something that fuels our defect, we give our defect power over us. In fact, Joshua takes Achan, and everything of Achan's, including the accursed spoils of Jericho, and stones them and then incinerates them. We too must pile those stones on, find the true facts that will destroy the desire to hold onto what will hurt us, and hurl them at the destructive tendency until it falls and is buried. We must completely destroy the spiritual culprits, burn them up with a zeal to do God's will. Don't feel sorry for Achan; he knew the penalty. Sometimes when the inner culprit is found, it looks like an innocent little problem, a minor fear, a simple want, a slight oversight. Don't believe it. It is often the little things we hold onto that often end up becoming the monsters in our lives. We must search them out and destroy them.

Spiritually speaking, when God says "Destroy all," he means it, and for good reason. Once the accursed things have been removed from our lives, we can go on to confront the other spiritual obstacles that remain before us. Now Joshua can go back to the city of Ai, and conquer it.

Ambush

God had instructed Joshua to lay an ambush against Ai. First, five thousand men should hide behind the city, between Ai and the city of Bethel. Then the rest were to approach the front, wait for the men of Ai to come out, and flee before them, drawing them away from the city in hot pursuit. When the men of Ai were far enough away, the men in hiding should come out and enter the city and burn it down. The Israelites followed God's plan and drew the men of Ai away from their city. When the Israelites in hiding came out and burned their city, the men of Ai looked back and lost heart. They became completely discouraged, having nothing left to fight for. They lost their strength and, once surrounded, were easily defeated.

In regard to our spiritual progress, there is an important lesson in this battle plan. Remember that the walls of the enemy cities can represent denials or excuses that protect our defects of character. In the case of Jericho, which represented a large character defect, the walls fell because, despite their apparent impregnability, they had a weakness. It's difficult to make up legitimate excuses for the really big evils of life. They don't hold up. We can't say, "Well, I like to beat up my spouse. It's good for my self-esteem." That type of excuse doesn't hold up for long. Or imagine saying, "Cheating on my spouse regularly keeps me in excellent physical condition." It's hard to make strong excuses for really blatant malevolence. Thus, the excuses for the blatant and noxious defects, represented by Jericho, easily crumble and expose the real enemy within. But the little and seemingly insignificant shortcomings symbolized by Ai don't. The excuses around these spiritual enemies are small but powerful. It's hard to fight some of these defects because they can seem so innocent and harmless.

For example, we might say to ourselves, "This doesn't really hurt anyone," "I'm really only hurting myself," or "Sometimes it's necessary to act that way." These shortcomings easily hide behind excuses because they don't seem that bad to us. We might say, "Feeling a little anger now and then isn't going to hurt anyone, as long as I don't express it" or "Sometimes it's necessary to complain and bicker" or "I have special sexual needs. I can't help but lust now and then. It's a good release." As long as we believe these excuses, and others like them, the enemy remains protected behind the walls of illusion.

The only way to beat these less obvious character defects is to draw the failing away from its excuse. Like Joshua drawing the men of Ai away from their city, we must see those defects for what they are, apart from their excuses. We've got to see that these little pests are out to kill us and are just as noxious as any other defect in our lives. Even as Joshua and his men first ran away from the men of Ai as part of their battle plan, we can step back and take a good look at what the defect is really like, recognize how it can beat us backward, and even begin to kill the good things we love. We must realize the real destruction this defect can cause. Once we realize this, and separate the defect from its excuses by drawing it out of hiding, it begins to lose its power over us.

When the men of Ai were drawn away, Joshua gave the signal for his men in hiding to enter the city and burn it down. It is interesting to note that they had been waiting near the city of Bethel, which means "House of God." A house symbolizes a way of thought. A house of God is a symbol of doctrine, spiritual truths that can pierce through false ideas and expose evil for what it is really. Full force, these Israelites come out of hiding near this city, enter Ai, and burn it. The truth has a way of dissipating false ideas. Like these warriors in ambush, we too must use the truth we know and burn down everything that supports our excuse-making. A woman suffering from mild cases of anger and resentment must say to herself, "Whom am I kidding? My anger hurts me badly. It burns me up. And I can't contain it. It may not explode onto people any more, but it comes out in bits and pieces all over the place in what

I do and say. This anger is worthless and a real enemy." A person with the desire to manipulate must say, "Bickering is just another form of manipulation. It's just a less subtle form. There is never an excuse to bicker and complain. I can talk of needs, but not harass and cajole." A man dealing with sexual issues might have to confess to himself, "Sexual fantasy is not as bad as the real thing, but it is clearly hurting my relationship with my partner. It isn't providing any release, but only making sexual tensions within me worse. If I want to really love, I've got to stop seeing sex as something selfish and dirty, and start giving. I've got to clean up my act." These are examples of separating our spiritual defects from their excuses and burning those excuses down.

When the warriors of Ai saw their city burning, they lost hope. They lost their will to live. The same is true in a spiritual sense. When we draw the defect away from the excuses, and absolutely destroy those excuses, the defect has no will to live and cannot help but vanish, for the only power any evil has in our lives is through its walls of denial and illusion. Burn them down and we can conquer any defect, no matter how great or how small, no matter how strong it may seem, or how deeply imbedded in our character. The defect melts away and is conquered.

After the defeat of Ai, Joshua built a new altar; there the congregation of Israel worshiped their God and renewed their covenant with him. We too, having now conquered several enemies of our spiritual lives, desire to renew our vows with our Maker. We recognize the amazing power of the Divine, and we see that we have made tremendous progress toward becoming a whole and complete human being. We feel a certain control over our lives that we had never before experienced. It is not a dysfunctional type of control, but a sense of creative power, direction, resolve. We realize that the power of God is working through us, within our own free choice, bringing us victory over our shortcomings, and leading us onward into greater joy and deeper peace.

Exercises

1. What defect of character have you so far only toyed with removing? How can you begin to send in all the troops to defeat this defect? Promise yourself that you will devote all your attention to removing this defect. Then pray to God to take this defect from you. Are you able to defeat it?

2. Take an inventory of your life in an area that needs work. What are the accursed things preventing you from making some progress in this area? Take action to remove them.

3. Examine a minor defect of character in your life. Draw it away from its walls by asking yourself, "How does this harm me?" Search for its destructive nature. What excuses cover this destructiveness? Burn those excuses down! Let the defect melt away.

READINGS

When the inhabitants of Gibeon heard what Joshua had done to Jericho and Ai, they worked craftily, and went and pretended to be ambassadors. And they took old sacks on their donkeys, old wineskins torn and mended, old and patched sandals on their feet, and old garments on themselves; and all the bread of their provision was dry and moldy. And they went to Joshua, to the camp at Gilgal, and said to him and to the men of Israel, "We have come from a far country; now therefore, make a covenant with us." . . . And Joshua said to them, "Who are you, and where do you come from?" So they said to him: "From a very far country your servants have come, because of the name of the Lord your God; for we have heard of his fame. . . . This bread of ours we took hot for our provisions from our houses on the day we departed to come to you. But now look, it is dry and moldy. And these wineskins which we filled were new, and see, they are torn; and these our garments and our sandals have become old because of the very long journey." Then the men of Israel took some of their provisions; but they did not ask counsel of the Lord. So Joshua made peace with them, and made a covenant with them to let them live. . . . And it happened at the end of three days, after they had made a covenant with them, that they heard that they were their neighbors who dwelt near them. But the children of Israel did not attack them, because the rulers of the congregation had sworn to them by the Lord God of Israel. And all the congregation murmured against the rulers. Then all the rulers said to all the congregation, "We have sworn to them by the Lord God of Israel; now therefore, we may not touch them. . . . Let them live, but let them be woodcutters and water carriers for all the congregation." . . . And that day, Joshua made them woodcutters and water carriers for the congregation and for the altar of the Lord, in the place which he would choose, even to this day.
Joshua 9:3-21, 27

CHAPTER ELEVEN

Making Peace with Shortcomings

Gibeonites

To chop wood means to place merit in the good works which one performs.

Arcana Coelestia 2784

Impostors

Joshua and Israel conquered one enemy after another, swiftly capturing the land of Canaan. In fact, Joshua's fame spread throughout the land among his enemies. The rest of the inhabitants of Canaan were struck with fear. They had reason to fear, because the Israelites were tearing through the countryside, sparing no one. They destroyed all and seemed truly invincible.

The Gibeonites, who were next in line to be wiped out by Israel, having five small cities just over the horizon from Ai, gathered to discuss their strategy. Apparently, at least one of them had a tremendously creative idea. He proposed that, since Israel was wiping out everyone in this land of Canaan that had been promised to them by their God, the Gibeonites should pretend that they were not from Canaan. He proposed that they send emissaries to Joshua dressed in old and worn clothes, with dried-up provisions, to tell Joshua that they represented a distant nation that would like to make a covenant of peace with Israel. Perhaps if these bogus ambassadors buttered Joshua up, promised to serve Israel, and pressed him to make a covenant, Joshua would spare them. They knew if the Israelites did make such a promise that, even when they discovered that the Gibeonites were not from a far land but enemies just over the hill, they would have to spare them, because people didn't break oaths back then. To break an oath meant disgrace and abandonment by their God.

The Gibeonites decided they had nothing to lose by following this plan. A group of them dressed up in old clothes and worn sandals. They carried dry and moldy bread, and old, mended wineskins. They came to the Israelite camp and bowed before Joshua and the elders of Israel. They explained that they were from a faraway land but had heard of the Israelites and their powerful God, and had come to make a covenant with them. They said they and the rest of the Gibeonites would serve Israel in any capacity, if only Israel would make a covenant of peace with them.

It's interesting that the elders of Israel first responded, "How do we know that you don't live on the other side of the hill?" But the Gibeonites showed them their old and crusty bread, their worn and mended wineskins, and their tattered clothes as proofs of their long journey. They continued to flatter the Israelites by telling them how great they were. Joshua and the elders of Israel, not taking counsel of God, quickly fell for the scheme and agreed they would not destroy the Gibeonites. They made a covenant of peace with them. The Gibeonites returned home, successful. Israel would not destroy them, even when they discovered they had been fooled.

It didn't take long for the Israelites to discover the truth. Imagine Joshua, sitting in his tent, reflecting on all his great victories and his renown, how even these people from a distant county had come to pay him homage. But then a messenger enters Joshua's tent with an embarrassed and frantic look about him. He tells Joshua, "Bad news. You know those ambassadors from a faraway land? They live not ten minutes from here on the other side of the hill!" Joshua, in a mild state of shock, realizes that he and the Israelites have been duped! And worse, there's nothing he can do about it.

The Israelites were upset, but they kept their promise. They did not destroy the Gibeonites, but they did subjugate them. They made all the Gibeonites water carriers and woodcutters, lifelong servants of Israel, even as they had promised in their covenant. As long as the Gibeonites obeyed, The Israelites would not harm them.

Spiritual Impostors

Like the other enemies in Canaan, the Gibeonites represent character defects that stand in our way. But they are not as harmful as some of our problems. In fact, these defects of character, like the Gibeonites, can appear to be our friends. The Gibeonites told the Israelites that they were not from Canaan, that they were not in the way of Israel receiving its inheritance. In the same way, certain of our defects of character feign friendliness, seem not to be in our way or to prevent us from enjoying a happy and spiritually healthy life. These defects flatter us. They claim to serve us, and they trick us into letting them live within us.

What would some of these Gibeonite-type defects be? Think about pride as an example. Isn't this one of the last defects to go? This particular defect starts flattering us, especially when we start changing our lives and doing some real good for people. Like the Gibeonites praising Joshua, pride praises us and tells us how great we are compared to others. Let's face it, most of us think we're smarter than others in certain areas. We think we know it all, or, at least, we think we know a lot. Pride can convince us that we are the best in our field, the smartest lawyer or doctor, the most competent teacher, the most caring counselor, the most loving parent, the hardest worker. In fact, that pride seems like an old friend, offering self-esteem and self-reliance to pull us through life. It tells us it is not the enemy, it is a friend who will only help us and makes us feel good about ourselves. When we hear this, we believe it. We let it slip by and continue to play a part in our character.

Another Gibeonite-type of defect that is often seen as a friend is what one might call "self-merit." It is the feeling that we can create our own heaven without God or a higher power. We believe that we build up and control our own lives, that we are the source of our own wisdom and power, and thus our own happiness. We accept credit for our good works. We might say to ourselves, "Look at the work that I have done! Look at the wonderful family I have raised! Look at all the people I have helped!" Like Joshua, we might even say, "Look at the enemies I have conquered!" But in reality we would still be wandering the spiritual wilderness without God. God gives us everything we have. Even if we build a great company, discover a cure for a debilitating disease, feed thousands of poor, raise the perfect children, it is God who has given us these blessings. But the Gibeonites within tell us that we are the grand masters of all that we do. Hearing that, we can tend to believe it; and like Joshua, we let those comforting feelings of self-merit and control live on, unchallenged and untouched.

Another example of a character flaw that simulates being a friend is the habit of interfering in other people's lives, being a busybody. Everybody suffers from this defect to some degree, and, like the Gibeonites, it can easily pretend to be a friend, even an asset to spiritual growth and life. This habit can dress itself up as a very harmless practice, hurting no one. In fact, it can even appear to be useful. We may believe that being a busybody actually teaches us a great deal about people and human nature. We might be tricked into believing that our interference comes from a genuine concern about our neighbor. We only want to help; we only want to serve. In reality, that tendency comes from a sick delight in exposing the weaknesses of others. Hardcore busybodies are spiritual voyeurs.

The Gibeonites didn't just tell the Israelites that they were not a threat. They claimed to come from a distant country. They demonstrated this with their dried and crusty bread, their old wineskins, and their worn clothes. These different pieces of false evidence specifically relate to our own lives.

The Gibeonites, upon being challenged by the elders of Israel to prove their identity, first produced moldy bread as evidence of their long journey. What does this bread symbolize? Remember the bread in the wilderness. This bread has the same significance. It represents goodness and delight. The Gibeonites' producing bread for the Israelites symbolizes how certain character defects seem to be able to produce some good in our lives. Upon examining these particular shortcomings, we can see that some good has come forth from our pride, for instance, or the sense of self-merit and control, or even from being a busybody. But interestingly, the bread is old and moldy, which too, is highly symbolic. Defects of character produce not genuine good but tainted good. In fact, sometimes we might view these Gibeonite-type defects as good only in the sense that they are "necessary evils." Take pride, for example. The good that it seems to produce is a sense of self-esteem or motivation to do a job well. These may not be the best motivating factors; sometimes the good they produce is a little moldy—we may become a tad arrogant or headstrong. But we are convinced that the defect is, ultimately, necessary. The same may be true with the desire to create our own world and control it. We realize this isn't the best mode of operation. Sometimes it is difficult to let go and relax, but this defect certainly seems to help us accomplish our goals. It seems a necessary way to operate. Even those who gossip or interfere in others' lives can point to times when it has actually benefitted others, though it is not the ideal way to communicate. This is the Gibeonites producing moldy bread as proof of their legitimacy.

The wineskins that the Gibeonites show the Israelites are old and patched, proof of a long and tedious journey. Those skins symbolize our own way of thinking, our doctrine of life, that holds the truth that we know. For instance, in Matthew 9:16-17, Jesus warned the disciples of John not to put new wine into old skins, lest they burst. That was a warning not to try to fit his new truth into the old and literalistic ways of the pharisees, but to search for new ways of thinking and living to encompass these truths. In this story of the Gibeonites, these worn skins symbolize a well-worn way of thinking that accompanies these defects of character. The old and patched skins testify that our way of thought has proved itself through years of experience. For instance, coming from a state of pride, we might pull out the old "wineskin" that symbolically states, "I've trusted in other people's judgment before and it never works. Self-reliance is absolutely necessary in my business." This attitude is well-worn and time-tested and contains what we think is some wholesome truth. In another instance, in a time of compulsive controlling, we might pull out the old, worn thought patterns that say, "If I don't control others, they will control me. I've seen it a hundred times. Control or be controlled! That's my motto!" And that goes for being a busybody as well. We might pull out an old argument we often use on ourselves that says, "Look at all I have learned about human beings, and how much I have helped others by involving myself in others' affairs." Like a torn wineskin, these arguments may not hold a lot of water, but we patch them over and keep using them. They look like very credible evidence for continuing to believe in the value of our old, well-worn defects.

As another part of their act, the Gibeonites wore old clothing. What does clothing represent in our spiritual lives? It isn't too different from what it represents in society today. Besides wearing what is comfortable or in fashion, we also wear clothes to make a statement about ourselves. Uniforms, for instance, indicate one's line of work. Public servants such as postal workers, police, and military personnel wear uniforms to link them with their particular duty or service. Metaphorically, clothing in the Bible symbolizes what a uniform does today. It symbolizes "service"—what one does to be useful. When the Gibeonites point to their well-worn clothes they are pointing to the apparent service these defects perform. They are well-tested means of serving us. At least that is what they tell us. Not only have pride, desire for control, and nosiness served us well throughout the years, but they have served others, too. Our pride may convince us that we stand as a role model. Our controlling defect tells us that we've led many people's lives in the right direction. Our nosiness tells us that we have helped people by unburdening them, and sympathizing with them. Our defects demonstrate that they are solid components of our spiritual lives, that we have counted on them and their faithful service for years.

We have discussed three defects of character in specific: pride, self-merit, and interference in others' lives. Your particular Gibeonites may be very different and tell different lies. They may be fears that swear to you they're legitimate. Your Gibeonite defects may seem passive, like laziness, melancholy, or resignation. You must discover the Gibeonites in your life for yourself. What apparently harmless character defect has been lying to you? Are you being lured into making a covenant with it?

Joshua's Mistake

What was Joshua's big mistake? Clearly, it was the same mistake that the Israelites had made repeatedly. One would think that the Israelites would have finally gotten the message, but we human beings can be quite thickheaded. Joshua didn't consult God. He judged these Gibeonites according to their appearance, not according to God's word.

We can do the same at times. Often we will judge according to appearance rather than what God tells us, especially in his revelation. The problem is that appearances are deceptive. That is why God has given us revelation, whether in the Bible, the Koran, the Bhagavad Gita, or other sacred texts. People need a source of truth outside of themselves and their own experience to guide them, to help them make good decisions about their spiritual lives. Without a spiritual source, such as one of the inspired texts or others like them, humans can be deceived by appearances and make some major mistakes. Like Joshua, if individuals judge only according to appearances, they can make covenants with tendencies within that are less than noble.

For example, what successful person in business would not believe that he or she was on the right track by acquiring great wealth and power? To all appearances, this seems like a great way to live and a goal to be desired. But the Bible tells us that, although we may gain the whole world, we may still lose our own souls. We are urged to look beyond the appearance to our motives. It's not what is outside a person that defiles the person, but what is inside. In fact, there is nothing wrong with becoming successful, rich, and powerful, as long as we don't sell our soul in order to achieve those goals. We can gain the whole world; but if we do so from a self-love, greed, contempt for others, or a desire to dominate, our inner world will fall apart. Spiritually, we will become destitute and poor. The appearance of success won't tell us that. Revelation tells us that. We all must ask ourselves what is motivating us to do the things we do, regardless of the outward appearance. Are we living up to the codes of religion and morality? If not, why not? Are we right, and everyone else wrong?

Joshua went on to make a covenant with the Gibeonites, and we too can make a covenant with certain shortcomings. Having overlooked their destructive nature, we unconsciously give them permission to dwell with us. We unconsciously say, "This part of my character is acceptable to me. I will let it become a part of my daily life." We may, for instance, accept pride as part of our character. We may accept certain fears as a part of us never to be shunned. A desire for control may be tolerable. Having made the covenant, the destructive tendency we have accepted tends to disappear deep within our unconscious, into the hills and valleys of our mind.

Even Enemies Can Serve

When Joshua discovered that the Gibeonites lived on the other side of the hill, he did not destroy them. Even though they had deceived him, he kept his promise and let them live. But he didn't let them rule themselves or do what they wanted. They became slaves of Israel.

Joshua's action, or lack of action, represents a significant shift in the patterns of what we have learned so far. The biblical narrative describes the Israelites as making a clean sweep of the land, destroying everything. But Joshua did not destroy the Gibeonites. They could not be destroyed without Joshua's breaking his oath and risking possible harm to himself. The Gibeonites were allowed to live, which symbolizes the fact that some of our shortcomings are never going to be wiped out completely. Some shortcomings have become so much a part of our character that they continue to dwell with us and remain a part of us the rest of our lives. This is especially true with such defects as pride and self-merit. These are often so much a part of our nature that God can't completely wipe them out without doing real damage to us. We relate so much to these deep-seated defects that without them we truly wouldn't be ourselves.

Granted, that seems like a tremendous contradiction—we are not to be duped by these defects into thinking that they can serve us, only to find out that they can serve us and, moreover, can never be destroyed. But the contradiction is only an appearance. We are commanded to fight each and every character defect within us, but we must realize that some of our defects will never be completely eradicated. But that doesn't mean they can't be vanquished. They can be stopped from ruling our lives. They can be subordinated in our thoughts and feelings. They can be made slaves.

Joshua did not destroy the Gibeonites, but he made them slaves. In relation to our character flaws, that might mean we will never completely do away with our pride. But we won't let it be the motivating factor in our lives anymore. We may always have some desire to map out and control our world, but it will never again rule us; thus, it will never destroy us, as it might have once long ago in our Egypt state of mind. On the other hand, it will never completely disappear. We will always have a little tendency here and there to grab on and control. God will use that, though; it will serve. And that is true for other deeply ingrained character defects as well.

The Gibeonites were made water carriers and woodcutters. These two services certainly provide some insight into how these lifelong defects might serve us. We know that the spiritual significance of water and wood are truth and goodness. Some defects, if they cannot be completely removed, can be made to serve us by bringing us some truth and good after all. Our pride, for instance, can be used by God to bring us both water and wood. It can, indeed, serve to help motivate us to work hard, or to be very precise in what we do, or to pursue learning with great zeal. Some of our motivation, in reality, may be selfish pride, but God uses it to help us learn and do well. As long as it doesn't rule us, it can serve.

In another instance, our desire for control, when it rules us, can destroy us; but when it plays a subservient role it can be useful to others. Part of that desire can fuel a leadership ability most people don't have. Perhaps we initially enjoy leading because of our desire to control, but God works with it, leading us to serve, rather than dominate others. Even our desire to interfere in other people's affairs, when it does not rule, can serve in a mediatory way. We may counsel, perform social work, or teach, where learning about others' difficulties is part of the service and not just a means of exposing people's frailties. We learn to listen in order to help. God can take that initial desire to be nosy and make it serve as a device for good listening in a useful setting such as counseling. And that is true for other defects as well. God is remarkable in his abilities. If he won't wipe out certain defects within us (because we couldn't handle it), he will turn them into servants that bring us both truth and good.

What does this mean overall in our spiritual development? It means that we should try to follow our God to the best of our ability in order to enter our own promised land. We can spy out the land well, look for character defects, and watch for deception. Remember, with God on our side, we can't fail. No defect of character can stand up to us because we rely on a power greater than any problem we might face, a power greater than ourselves. Sometimes we will get discouraged. We will find that certain defects have pretended to be our lifelong friends and we have made them welcome. We might recognize that some of these flaws will remain and play a small role in our lives. God tells us this so that we will not become discouraged, so we won't spend the rest of our lives wondering why we still have that touch of pride or that inkling to control, or why we still get a bit of delight when we hear other people's problems. We simply admit that we're not perfect. Only God is perfect, and we'll never be God. We may never completely overcome these defects, but at least they will never rule us. God takes our shortcomings and makes them of service to us and to our neighbor.

Final Conquests

After subduing the Gibeonites, the Israelites systematically defeated the rest of their enemies. Five enemy kings confronted them at one time, but Joshua and his armies defeated them. In fact, we are told in Joshua 10 that the sun stood still until the enemy was defeated. Even in our lives, the spiritual sun will always stand still for us. God's love and wisdom, his warmth and light, will shine down on us, even during spiritual battle, to give us victory over our oppressors. One by one, the enemies will fall, and we will inherit the promised land.

To describe the Israelites' sweeping victories that followed their treaty with the Gibeonites, I quote a passage from Joshua (10:28-32) describing some of these first victories in southern Canaan. Joshua later went on to conquer the north as well. Think of these enemies as character defects that will fall before the fighting truth within you. Think about inheriting the good land, even as Israel did, once these enemies have been removed, for that, in a spiritual sense, is what this story is all about:

> On that day Joshua took Makkedah, and struck it and its king with the edge of the sword. He utterly destroyed them. . . . Then Joshua passed from Makkedah, and all Israel with him, to Libnah; and they fought against Libnah. And the Lord delivered it and its king into the hand of Israel; he struck it and all the people who were in it with the edge of the sword. . . . Then Joshua passed from Libnah, and

all Israel with him to Lachish; and they encamped against it and fought against it. And the Lord delivered Lachish into the hand of Israel, who took it on the second day. . . .

This description of one victory after another continues until we are told, "So Joshua conquered all the land: the mountain country and the South and the lowland and the wilderness slopes, and all their kings; he left none remaining" (Joshua 10:40).

These conquests symbolize the conquests we will most certainly have over the spiritual enemies within us. Once we get rolling, nothing can stop us. Like Joshua, we will experience one victory after another, one success after another. Even as the children of Israel, we will fully and completely seize our spiritual inheritance from our enemies and win for ourselves a prosperous land, a land flowing with milk and honey.

Exercises

1. Which defects of character display the moldy bread, old skins, and worn clothes, as proofs of their right to exist in your life? Identify them and take steps to subdue them. How can they begin to serve you?

2. In times of doubt or temptation, don't just act on impulse. Appearances can deceive you. Ask yourself, "What does God say about this? Am I willing to forgo the appearance and do what God says?"

READINGS

So the Lord gave to Israel all the land of which He had sworn to give to their fathers, and they took possession of it and dwelt in it. The Lord gave them rest all around, according to all that He had sworn to their fathers. And not a man of all their enemies stood against them; the Lord delivered all their enemies into their hand. Not a word failed of any good thing which the Lord had spoken to the house of Israel. All came to pass.   Joshua 21:43-45

Now it came to pass, a long time after the Lord had given rest to Israel from all their enemies round about, that Joshua . . . called for all Israel . . . and said to them: "I am old, advanced in age. You have seen all that the Lord your God has done to all these nations because of you, for the Lord our God is he who has fought for you. . . . The Lord has driven out from before you great and strong nations; but as for you, no one has been able to stand against you to this day. One man of you shall chase a thousand, for the Lord your God is He who fights for you, as He has promised you. . . . And if it seems evil to you to serve the Lord, choose for yourselves this day whom you will serve. . . . But as for me and my house, we will serve the Lord." So the people answered and said: "Far be it from us that we should forsake the Lord and serve other gods; for the Lord our God is He who brought us and our fathers up out of the land of Egypt, from the house of bondage, who did those great signs in our sight, and preserved us in all the way that we went and among all the people through whom we passed. And the Lord drove out from before us all the people, even the Amorites, who dwelt in the land. We also will serve the Lord, for He is our God."   Joshua 23:1-10; 24:15-18

CHAPTER TWELVE

Spirituality

Peace in the Land

Peace in the heavens is the divine inmostly filling all the good there
with bliss, and this is where heavenly joy comes from.

Heaven and Hell 286

Spiritual Prosperity

We are told in Joshua 21:43-45, "The Lord gave them rest all
around, according to all that He had sworn to their fathers. And not
a man of all their enemies stood against them; the Lord delivered all
their enemies into their hand. Not a word failed of any good thing
which the Lord had spoken to the house of Israel. All came to pass."

Imagine one of the children of Israel plowing his field near his
new home in Canaan. Perhaps his children play in the grass beside
the house, while his wife works in the garden nearby. The sun is
bright, the sky is clear, and a morning dove sings a melody of peace
in a nearby fruit tree, giving the farmer a sense of calm and contentment. He notices that his plowshare has begun to loose itself
from the plow, and he bends down to fix it. He examines the hammer marks on the smooth metal and quickly calls to mind that this
plowshare used to be his sword. It had protected him for many
years and helped him and his people capture the promised land for
themselves. But now its use has changed. There is no enemy, at least
not nearby. There is no threat of war, or sneak attack, or violence
of any kind. He had beaten his sword into a farming tool. No longer
does it ward off the enemy, but rather it now breaks open the
ground so that seeds can be planted and crops can grow. Examining

197

that plowshare allows him to pause for a moment, to lean up against his plow and look across the vast horizon in wonder.

He remembers well where he had been, how he and his family fought for existence in the wilderness on the other side of the Jordan. He remembers the relentless days, the hot sun, the hunger and thirst, how much the bread and water from God meant to him and his family then. Now they eat and drink like royalty! He remembers with gladness the battles his people fought, how God was always there when they called upon him, how the enemy would always be vanquished.

Looking far beyond the horizon, he remembers, with thankfulness and relief, what his parents had taught him about their plight in Egypt. His father told them of the heavy burdens the Egyptians laid on the people, how pharaoh was a tyrant who ordered the death of Israel's sons. He remembers his father's words, "O how we cried." But he knows well that God heard the cry of his fathers and delivered them from Egypt. They walked out of Egypt unharmed. They crossed the Red Sea. They followed a pillar of cloud by day and fire by night, were fed in the wilderness, saw God on a mountain, and crossed into a new land promised to them from the beginning. Now that promise had been fulfilled. "Not a word failed of any good thing which the Lord had spoken to the house of Israel. All came to pass" (Joshua 21:43-45). A smile breaks forth on his face, and he bends down to fix his farming equipment. It looks like it's going to be a good year for the crops. It looks like it's going to be a handful of good years!

We are all that farmer. This time of peace symbolizes the spiritual peace and prosperity that can and will be ours. Yes, there will be challenges ahead. Israel still had work to do to keep the land from surrounding enemies. We also know that this biblical narrative continues into the stories of Judges, Samuel, Kings, and Prophets. Israel becomes a nation with a long history of challenge and development in this new land. This is typical of the true human situation. We never reach spiritual perfection, but we do reach a state of spiritual progress. We experience a rebirth, and we continue to grow.

This time of peace for Israel is real and is a real symbol of our rebirth into spirituality. Though there are challenges ahead of us, there will come a time in our lives when we have taken the land for our own, come into a new and spiritually healthy state of mind, a time of spiritual peace and prosperity. We too will beat our swords into plowshares. Those fighting truths represented by that sword have served us well in cutting through the false pretexts of our inner foes, rendering them harmless. Now the enemies have retreated to the borders of our consciousness. No longer do we suffer at their hands. And now those same truths that once fought for us help us to plow the ground of our conscious minds. They help us to plant new seeds of growth, which will bring forth wholesome fruit and grain for years to come.

We can pause to reflect on what the Divine has done for us. We remember well the spiritual battles within, the times of fear and lack of trust in God, when we thought all was hopeless, when God somehow pulled us through. We remember well the hunger and thirst in our spiritual wilderness. We remember the bondage of following our egos, the compulsion, the burdens, the sickness and pestilence, all of which seems so far away now. And it is so far away now. In fact, in some ways we wonder whether those past days of grief did not belong to someone else. Perhaps that was as we were, but we have been reborn. We have learned to trust in God, to take what is given to us, and to fight and defeat those inner enemies who would afflict us. That struggle is all over now. That pain, that dry emptiness, that solitude, that barren feeling of useless waste is no more. We own the land! We reap its fruits! We live in peace! We are not alone! God has done it all for us and will continue to be with us and bless us for as long as we allow him to—forever, if we choose.

Spiritual Rest

We are told in Joshua 21:44 that "the Lord gave them rest all around." This represents the rest the Divine will give us when we have reached our own promised land. But what kind of rest will we finally receive?

Some people think that the goal of spiritual development is to stop working. How many people picture heaven as a paradise to lounge around in all day, smelling the flowers and catching a few rays between naps? People also picture their heavenly existence as sitting on fluffy clouds, strumming a harp while singing songs of praise. Would you really want to go there? Even lazing around in a paradise would soon become boring. A heavenly life begins with an active life, and it begins right now. As Jesus said in Luke 17:21, "The kingdom of God is within you."

When we finally inherit that new life of spirituality, we won't be sitting on any clouds. We'll be active and useful, helping others in any way we can. In our homes, in our occupations, in our social lives, love will blossom forth into action. It will show itself in our relationship with our spouse, our children, our friends and acquaintances. It will take the form of a smiling face, a helping hand, an open ear, open arms. Even as the Israelites, after taking the land, began the work of sowing and reaping, building cities, governing, and living, we will begin to rebuild our lives. We will sow good seeds of new thoughts and ideas that will spring forth into action. We will build new strong and healthy ways of thinking. We will forge new relationships based on spiritual values and discover new means to serve ourselves and others. We will establish a new form of self-government: no dictatorial ego will rule over us and hurt us; our judgments will be made by free and rational thought. With God as our ruler and our final counsel, we will live life to the fullest.

We will also experience a certain inner rest that we never knew before. We will no longer suffer through excruciating battles with our destructive tendencies. The kind of rest that Israel received was rest from fighting its enemies. We will find rest from the inner battles we have fought each day for so long. Think of a problem you battle regularly right now, perhaps a bad habit, a compulsion, or a way of thinking. Imagine: someday that battle will be over. That problem will be gone, and with it, the tremendous labor you undertook to remove it from your life.

I remember Bob telling me that, while he suffered from a compulsive fear, he used to stare at other people and wonder how they could be content. He said, "Really, I used to stare at my boss in our meetings and wonder how this guy could be so happy. It was something I never knew." He wondered whether the concept of happiness was a joke. Later, after becoming involved in several self-help programs, including one for children of dysfunctional families, Bob discovered the origin and roots of his fears: he was afraid of failure. He fought a series of mental battles that lasted months in order to break a persistent fear. It was a tiring process. The fear kept returning, and Bob struggled to turn it over to God and allow God to care for him. Slowly Bob was able to conquer his fear.

Much later, after living without his compulsive fear, it suddenly dawned on him. He was sitting in a lounge chair in his backyard, with one eye on some burgers on the grill and the other on some beautiful cloud formations in the sky, when he realized that he was actually happy. Suddenly, it occurred to him that he had been experiencing this wonderful feeling for a couple of months. He said to himself, "So this is what others have been feeling all this time. So this is happiness." He said it felt great. The best thing about it was that, "It just felt like a mild pleasantness and sense of inner rest."

Another close acquaintance of mine, Lynn, said that she had worked hard for about a year and a half to stop some of her codependent ways of thinking and behaving with her husband. She had a terrible time battling her sense of martyrdom, taking on her husband's problems and then blaming him for giving her those problems. She fought hard not to push her will on him, as she was used to doing. After a long, tough series of battles to let him be himself and pass or fail life on his own terms, rather than hers, she let go. "In fact," she said, "When I look back to where I was two years ago and the kind of thinking and behaving I did back then, I can't believe it was me. I've changed so much. It was a lot of work, but I will never be that awful person again." She doesn't even have to battle those unhealthy thoughts and tendencies. They are vanquished. She lives a contented life now, involved with her family and part-time occupation, and she says her marriage is on a steady climb upward.

Rest from inner battles can and will come. Happiness is not a joke. If you are reading this from the wilderness, during your struggle with the Amalekites; or if you are fighting other spiritual enemies like those of Jericho or Ai; if you are growing weary of the battles, take heart. As God said to Joshua, "Be strong and of a good courage. Do not be afraid, nor be dismayed" (Joshua 1:9). You will find rest. If you can learn to trust in the Divine and, like Israel, fight the good fight, you will find rest for your soul. Finding the spiritual life takes work, but it culminates in spiritual rest. For indeed, as we have been told before, for six days out of seven we must work hard to create a new way of life for ourselves; but on the seventh day we will rest. And that seventh day never ends, once we come to it. A perpetual Sunday afternoon? Certainly, but a very useful one as well!

Spiritual Peace

Rest from spiritual battles clearly indicates a state of peace. But the type of peace that comes from a spiritual life exceeds the mere cessation of inner struggle or toil. The peace of the promised land is such a beautiful sense of calm, serenity, and inner tranquility that its precise description is elusive. We can only suggest it. Think of the feelings the Israelites experienced after all the search, struggle, and turmoil were over. Imagine their sense of relief, their sense of fulfillment, their sense of the real presence of God in their lives. This is the kind of relief we will feel upon reaching our desired state of spirituality. We may even sense it now on occasion, but there will come a time when it will never go away; it will last forever and even grow deep within our hearts.

To capture the sense of the inward peace we can experience, it would be useful to make a few comparisons.

Many of us remember our feelings when we heard the words "The war is over," whether that war was one of the world wars, Korea, Vietnam, or the Gulf War. The sense of utter relief and elation that accompanied those words is something to cherish. Not only did soldiers experience joy and elation at the news, but so did those whom each soldier had left behind at home. Mothers, fathers, sisters, brothers, wives, lovers, and friends wept for joy, hearing the news of their loved one's impending return home and the end of the terror. Some even danced in the streets.

On a spiritual plane, we can know a similar sense of joy and relief. The terror will be over for us as well, the terror of ourselves and our own destructive tendencies, of life and its uncertainties, of our day-to-day battles. One day we can realize these feelings are no more. We can rejoice inwardly when, within our inner spirit, we quietly realize, "The war is over."

This spiritual peace can also be compared to our experience with nature. For instance, have you survived a terrible storm? Remember that sense of peace after the storm? I remember it well. My parents owned a summer house on the beach in New Jersey, and every time we heard that a hurricane was going to hit the coast, my father and I would leave our home near Philadelphia and travel two hours to the shore house to board up the place. Sometimes, Dad let me stay there with him to ride out the storm. It was risky, but we survived, and I learned a lot from the experience. What I learned or appreciated the most was experiencing the incredible calm after the storm.

One time, just as the wind reached its peak, howling through the cracks in the wooden planks we had hammered up against the windows for protection, as the rain and hail came to its most intense rhythmic pounding on the roof and walls, and we heard the tremendous ocean waves crashing against the bulkhead, twisting the front steps that led down to what used to be a beach but was now a torrent of rushing water, the storm broke up. Just as I wondered whether my dad was crazy for bringing us down there and thought we just might be washed away by the storm, the screaming winds grew silent. The rain and hail slowed to a gentle rapping and ceased. Soon, even the waves took on a friendly lapping sound, as I listened through the boarded windows. We waited a half hour, perplexed at this sudden change. But then Dad's face grew bright. "It's over!" he exclaimed with an expression of curiosity and delight.

We walked out the door facing the street to survey the damage and to explore the eerie silence. Two telephone poles lay fallen in the street. They reminded me of fresh blades of tall grass cut down with a sickle. The roof of a house a half-block south was torn off and hung over the neighbor's garage. Bits and pieces of every-thing—glass, tile, plastic, and wood—lay all over place. It looked as if the block had been bombed. We walked beside our house, through a small stream of water under which was a sidewalk, toward the bulkhead and the dark, frightening ocean. The water had torn our steps in two, but the bulkhead had held, and the tide had actually begun to recede.

I remember the profound silence, the stillness in the midst of such destruction. I looked up with amazement at a small patch of clear blue sky and the first sign of stars as night fell. Seeing the ocean receding, soaking in the silence, feeling the cool rain water, gently running through my toes as it drained off the walkway, soothed my entire being. I felt such a sense of relief, but also wonder about it all. The violent storm had ended and was replaced by a natural tran-quility. Also, our house had fared well, and fortunately so did we.

This type of peace is analogous to spiritual peace. You and I might have lived through a time of confusion, howling fears, mixed-up thoughts, waves of uncontrollable emotions, pounding guilt or dismay on the roofs of our minds. But holding fast to what is right, and especially building our lives on the firm foundation of genuine faith in a power greater than ourselves, we not only sur-vive but experience a deep peace never felt before. All the turmoil, fear, confusion, and desperation come to an end. The sense of dev-astation trickles to a halt and ceases. It is replaced with a soothing calm—serenity.

Mothers know the wonderful sense of calm, accomplishment, and joy at the birth of their child. Fathers can know it vicariously. At the birth of each of our four children, like many husbands do today with their wives, I was Cathy's birthing partner. Even though I spent much nervous energy watching the fetal monitor between contractions, helping Cathy with her special breathing during labor, and generally getting in the nurse's way, I was struck by the look on Cathy's face as she reached transition. I had never seen such determination. As she panted, breathed, pushed, panted, breathed pushed . . . , an inner strength suddenly appeared and flooded into her face. I am told that with some mothers there is a period during the actual labor when life and death meet. They come to a point when they may be tempted to give up and fall back into the darkness, and that is when they must persevere the most. Perhaps this is a midwife's tale, but a midwife told me that some mothers, though few, do give up and actually go into shock and even die. Cathy clearly had met the challenge and chose life, life not only for herself but for that infant within her. She continued full strength.

Soon our child appeared in the doctor's gentle hands, followed by a tiny body that shook with the thrill of the first sensation of life itself. This was followed by a good healthy wail. A new soul had been born, another son.

As our tiny child was placed in his mother's bare arms, I was struck again by the look on Cathy's face. That look of sheer determination was gone. It had been replaced with delight. That inner strength had also disappeared. She looked absolutely exhausted, which, indeed, she was; but the strength had turned into an unmistakable inner peace and tranquility. The labor had been greater than anything she had ever known or experienced, but she had endured and brought forth life, a new human being from her very self!

Only women can truly know and understand that experience. But spiritually, we can all experience a similar type of inner tranquility and joy, at the new birth that takes place within us. Each of us works through a type of labor, struggling against the darkness and weakness of our own minds and hearts. We push forward, not simply because God has told us to, but in order to produce life. It is an intense labor, as we work to bring forth a new life for ourselves. We can summon an inner strength to pull us through. A power greater than ourselves comes over us and floods into our being. We begin the creative process of a rebirth or regeneration of our own selves. Suddenly we realize the purpose of the labor. During all this time of turmoil, we didn't struggle for nothing. The final result is something more positive, more fulfilling, more wonderful than we ever imagined or dreamed. It is a miracle! From our spiritual labor and struggle has come forth a new life. We cherish that life, hold it in our arms, full of a healthy sense of pride, confidence, deep peace, and pure love. That life is ours to have and to hold forever, innocent, tender, peaceful, heavenly.

I personally sense this peace in nature. Sometimes I sense a feeling analogous to spiritual peace quite apart from struggle. I have enjoyed it in the gentle colors of a sunrise on a lovely spring day or in the myriads of glittering stars on a clear August night. I have explored it walking down a mountain path, following a trickling stream of pure spring water as it dances between and around the rocks and pebbles. I have heard it gently whisper through the leaves and branches of the trees on a cool summer evening. I have inhaled it in the salty ocean air, or from a high mountaintop, or in the thick, cool air of a rain forest. I have touched it in the warm hand of a loved one, in a gentle hug, a loving kiss. I have sensed it all around at times. It permeates nature and even lives beyond it. Perhaps you have sensed it too?

Our experience of this type of peace only comes because we have the capacity for the spiritual peace within. If we did not know that peace, or at least have the ability to know it, we would not recognize the beauty of the sunrise, the call of the wind in the trees or on the ocean, or the peace within a special touch. As we struggle to reach the promised land, spiritual peace comes to us through these experiences. Nature, human interaction, and the experience of living become meaningful. Peace, love, tranquility, and inner meaning can be sensed in all experiences, because we allow them to affect us. We open our senses to these things. All of God's creation becomes a living source of spiritual peace and joy.

Spiritual Power

After Israel had soundly secured their land, Joshua spoke to them with words of encouragement. One of the promises Joshua made to the children of Israel was this: "One man of you shall chase a thousand [enemies], for the Lord your God is He who fights for you, as He has promised you" (Joshua 9:10). "One man" of Israel was not this powerful over his enemies just because he had tried to improve himself. He didn't carry any formidable weapons or work out with weights or learn self-defense. To all appearances he looked the same. But he could chase a thousand enemies away because he truly relied on a power greater than himself. The Lord his God was with him and gave him that power.

The same is true in our spiritual lives. You and I can come to a point when we will be able to chase our own inner spiritual enemies away. Our defects of character will flee before us. When we reach a strong and secure state of spirituality, temptation to return to one defect or another may rise, but it won't last long. With the slightest effort we will be able to chase that temptation away. One true thought will be able to chase a thousand false thoughts away. One good feeling will cause a thousand bad ones to flee from our presence. We can experience incredible spiritual power over our destructive tendencies.

Consider that. We may once have suffered from deadening guilt. We conquered that perception, and those thoughts no longer rule or play any significant part in our lives. But even if they did try to return, as negative thoughts will do from time to time, we would be able to cast them out with ease. Because we rely on a power greater than self, we are able to see with a new perspective that these thoughts only lead to useless pain, that we don't need or want them, and that they must immediately cease. And remarkably enough, they do stop, instantly.

Perhaps, after we inherit a sense of spirituality, old feelings of self-pity try to rear their ugly heads and re-enter our lives. With God's power clearly working for us, we are able to confront those feelings before they can take hold; and without even flashing a sword, they retreat. We think, "No, I reject that self-pity. I will not accept it back into my life." Amazingly enough, it quickly retreats without even a fight. And so all defects of character will retreat.

We can disarm even those Amalekites that used to sneak up and surprise us. We anticipate them before they can enter our conscious minds. We stop them dead in their tracks. We recognize the lies that once ambushed us at every turn. We just don't buy them anymore. We say to ourselves, "No way will I fall back into that trap. There is absolutely no way!" So we remain free from inner strife, with a clear head, clear conscience, and a sense of spiritual power beyond compare.

A woman from a self-help group that I've been involved with freely discussed her feeling of power over at least one of her destructive tendencies. She said she could clearly see that God had removed rage from her life. She used to repress her anger and frustration over marital and child-raising issues, and then erupt in anger at her children. But through conscious work on her problem, she conquered it. She learned to process her feelings appropriately, to place her problems in God's care, not to act impulsively from her destructive tendency. Her rage went away. From time to time, she still feels the tendency begin to flare up. After all, cultivating a good marriage and raising children aren't easy for anyone. But when she feels this tendency begin to grow, she immediately confronts it and deals with it. She examines the building rage, asks herself why she feels that way and how it can be alleviated. She reminds herself that to act on this feeling will cause more trouble than it's worth. She refuses to submit to it, and the feeling quickly dissipates. She has noticed that in relating to her children, her tolerance level itself has been raised. She feels her family life is now in balance and under control.

You and I can achieve this sense of power over destructive tendencies in all that we do. Realistically, we will be tempted to return to old habits from time to time, but we can counter those destructive tendencies very quickly. Even the Israelites still had to deal with neighboring enemies and a few pockets of resistance here and there. But they were told that if they continued to rely on their God's power, one man could truly chase away a thousand foes. We will meet some resistance as we enjoy a new life of spirituality. But with the power of God, we'll be able to chase even a thousand destructive thoughts and tendencies away. They will have no power over us.

Spiritual Inheritance

God had promised the children of Israel that they would return to the land of their fathers and claim their inheritance. That promise was fulfilled. They returned to that paradise known to their forefathers and foremothers. But this time there was a difference. Even when their ancestors had lived in Canaan, they remained sojourners; the land was never really their own. But now, after securing the land, the Israelites could clearly call this land their home.

Spiritually, we return to a type of paradisal state of mind similar to that of childhood. We don't become ignorant again or naive or silly. But we do recapture that innocence and tenderness of childhood. As Jesus said, "Whoever does not receive the kingdom of God as a little child will by no means enter it" (Luke 18:17). We truly become as children. Our newly found innocence is one of wisdom. We follow because we know we should. We trust because we have learned to trust. We dream because it's right to dream. We play because we've known the burden of labor. We accept what comes, not because we are ignorant of the future, but because we are wise from the past. We trust that God will provide. Whether goodness or evil comes our way, God will provide and lead us to a closer union with him. We become willing to follow our God, which is true innocence. To become as little children once again, spiritually, is to trust absolutely in God. This is the return to our promised land, to an inner serenity that can be enjoyed here on earth.

The children of Israel also found themselves in a land and under a government that was truly their own. Compare the days when they were in Egypt to the days ahead in the promised land. From being slaves in a strange land, they had become self-governing lords of their own territory. Spiritually, the same is true with us. We feel at home in this new way of life. Maybe we feel that we are at home with ourselves for the first time in our lives. We feel alive, vibrant, free! Like Israel, we have escaped from bondage, from that old and destructive way of living. Now we rule our own lives from a full sense of self-determination. We don't act on egotistical whims or destructive impulses. We don't act from fear and inner compulsion. We freely choose our life's direction with wisdom based on love. We act wisely from a deep sense of love and commitment to life itself—to God, to our neighbor, and to ourselves. We have been delivered from the "house of bondage" and set free to enjoy our new home on the promised land.

Remember that God had promised Israel a land flowing with milk and honey. Milk and honey represent the highest forms of happiness. They symbolize heavenly and spiritual delight. You might recall that the manna in the wilderness also symbolized a type of delight but one that brought only a barely perceptible sense of happiness and contentment. The manna ceased when we entered the promised land. It was replaced by open and quite perceptible delights symbolized by the many fruits of the land, the figurative milk and honey. Ultimately our lives won't just feel sort of nice inside, vaguely rewarding. We're going to feel great! And why not? Isn't that what God wants? Of course it is. Our happiness will be genuine, healthy, and enduring. We will have fun!

There is nothing wrong with fun. If you can believe it, God created us for that very purpose. God, being Love itself, created us as objects and receiving vessels of his love. He desires nothing more than to love us, bless us, and fill us with all the joy and delight we are able to receive. When we enter the state represented by the promised land, we become open to receive his blessings. When we open our hearts, we open the doors to the most magnificent experience of all time and eternity. For when we open our hearts, God enters. Thus, the purpose of creation becomes fulfilled; we are made happy by Love itself, and we and Love become one.

Whom Shall We Serve?

Joshua left the children of Israel with a challenge: if they continued to follow their God, they would have good success; and if they did not, they would fail. He then asked them directly whom they would serve. He added that as for himself and his family, they would serve God. That is the challenge the fighting truth, represented by Joshua, places before us. It is the fundamental rule of life. Whom shall we serve? Are we ready to leave Egypt? Are we ready to walk that wilderness? Do we desire that promised land, with all our heart, mind, and strength? And once we have it, are we caring enough to keep it? Whom shall we serve? This is an essential question, perhaps the most profound question we can ask ourselves.

The children of Israel cried out their response to Joshua. It is a response that embodied the memory of the terror of Egypt, the years of struggle in the wilderness, the many battle wounds suffered to obtain a promise made long ago. Their response carried the memory of a people now reborn into a nation devoted to their God. We too carry this response within our hearts, after we have weathered our journey to paradise and returned to the promised land. With the words recorded in Joshua 24:16-18 and with the children of Israel, whose journey from bondage to freedom represents our own, we can finally proclaim with joy:

> Far be it that we should forsake the Lord . . . for the Lord our God
> is he who brought us and our fathers up out of the land of Egypt,

from the house of bondage, who did those great signs in our sight, and preserved us in all the way that we went. . . . We will also serve the Lord, for he is our God.

Exercises

1. List the good things that you have received from God, including not only the earthly benefits, but also spiritual ones such as peace of mind, times of happiness and contentment, etc.

2. Take the list to a quiet place—a church, a garden, a favorite spot in the woods. In that place, vocally thank God for each thing on that list. How does that make you feel?

3. If you haven't already set out, how can you begin your journey toward the promised land? Find a private place and kneel in prayer. Say to God, "As for me, I will serve you, for you are my God."

Bibliography

Bayley, Jonathan. *From Egypt to Canaan*. London: New Church Press, 1912.

De Charms, George. *Growth of the Mind*. Bryn Athyn, Pennsylvania: The Academy Book Room, 1953.

Dole, Anita S. *Bible Study Notes*. Boston: American New Church Sunday School Association, 1976.

Kline, Thomas L. *The Journey of Life*. Bryn Athyn, Pennsylvania: General Church Press, 1989.

Odhner, Hugo LJ. *The Divine Allegory*. New York: Swedenborg Foundation, 1954.

Swedenborg, Emanuel. *Arcana Coelestia*, 12 vols. Trans. John Clowes. Rvd. and Ed. John F. Potts. New York: Swedenborg Foundation, 1905-1910; rpt. 1995- .

Worcester, William. *The Sower*. Boston: American New Church Sunday School Association, 1951.

Wright, Theodore F. *The Spiritual Exodus*. Boston: Massachusetts New Church Union, 1905.